Word 2019 Beginner

WORD ESSENTIALS 2019 BOOK 1

M.L. HUMPHREY

SELECT TITLES BY M.L. HUMPHREY

WORD ESSENTIALS 2019

Word 2019 Beginner

Word 2019 Intermediate

POWERPOINT ESSENTIALS 2019

PowerPoint 2019 Beginner

PowerPoint 2019 Intermediate

EXCEL ESSENTIALS 2019

Excel 2019 Beginner

Excel 2019 Intermediate

Excel 2019 Formulas & Functions

Excel 2019 Formulas and Functions Study Guide

ACCESS ESSENTIALS 2019

Access 2019 Beginner

Access 2019 Intermediate

CONTENTS

INTRODUCTION   1

BASIC TERMINOLOGY   3

ABSOLUTE BASICS   11

BASIC TASKS   17

TEXT FORMATTING   23

PARAGRAPH FORMATTING   35

OTHER TIPS & TRICKS   55

FILE OPTIONS CUSTOMIZED SETTINGS   73

FILE INFO   81

PAGE FORMATTING   85

PRINTING   91

CONCLUSION   97

CONTROL SHORTCUTS   99

INDEX   101

ABOUT THE AUTHOR   105

Introduction

The purpose of this guide is to introduce you to the basics of using Microsoft Word 2019. While there are a number of other word processing programs out there, Word is still the gold-standard go-to program in use in large portions of the corporate world, so if you're going to be involved in a white collar job (and even some blue collar jobs), being familiar with Word will be a significant advantage for you. And essential for many jobs. (The days of having an assistant who could do those things for you are gone.)

Word at its most basic is incredibly simple to use. You open a new file, type in your text, save, and done.

But chances are you'll want control over the appearance of what you type. Maybe you need to use a different font or font size. Maybe you want to indent your paragraphs. Or include a bulleted or numbered list.

That's where this guide comes in. First I will walk you through the absolute basics (open, save, delete) but then most of this guide will be focused on what to do with your text once it's been typed into your document.

Having said that I'm not going to cover everything you can do in Word. The goal of this guide is to get you up to speed and comfortable with what you'll need for probably 98% of what you'll use Word for on a daily basis.

Some of the exceptions to that are if you're working in an environment where you need to use track changes with a group of users or you need to create something like tables or complex multilevel lists. Those are more advanced topics that are covered in *Word 2019 Intermediate*.

The goal here is to give you a solid foundation that you can work from.

As noted in the title and above, this book is written using Word 2019. I previously wrote a book, *Word for Beginners*, that was written using Word 2013 and was written to be generic enough that any user of Word could learn the basics from it. But this guide is written specifically for Word 2019, so I'm not going to mention what wasn't possible in older version of Word, for example.

As a beginner it probably won't matter. Where it becomes more relevant is at the intermediate level. But just so you know. The focus in this guide is Word 2019.

Alright then. Let's get started with some basic terminology.

Basic Terminology

Before we get started, I want to make sure that we're on the same page in terms of terminology.

Tab

I refer to the menu choices at the top of the screen (File, Home, Insert, Design, Layout, References, Mailings, Review, View, and Help) as tabs. If you click on one you'll see that the way it's highlighted sort of looks like an old-time filing system like below with the Home tab.

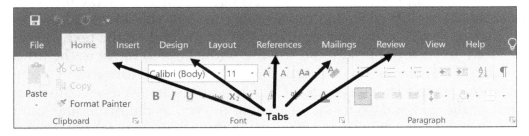

Each tab you select will show you different options.

For example, in the image above, I have the Home tab selected and you can do various tasks such as cut/copy/paste, format paint, change the font, change the formatting of a paragraph, apply a style to your text, find/replace words in your document, or select the text in your document. Other tabs give other options.

Click

If I tell you to click on something, that means to use your mouse (or trackpad) to move the arrow on the screen over to a specific location and left-click or right-click on the option. (See the next definition for the difference between left-click and right-click).

If you left-click, this generally selects an item. If you right-click, this generally creates a dropdown list of options to choose from. If I don't tell you which to do, left- or right-click, then left-click.

Left-Click/Right-Click

If you look at your mouse or your trackpad, you generally have two flat buttons to press. One is on the left side, one is on the right. If I say left-click that means to press down on the button on the left. If I say right-click that means press down on the button on the right.

Not all track pads have left- and right-hand buttons. In that case, you'll basically want to press on either the bottom left-hand side of the track pad or the bottom right-hand side of the trackpad. Since you're working blind it may take a little trial and error to get the option you want.

Select or Highlight

If I tell you to select text, that means to left-click at the end of the text you want to select, hold that left-click, and move your cursor to the other end of the text.

Another option is to use the Shift key. Go to one end of the text you want to select. Hold down the shift key and use the arrow keys to move to the other end of the text. If you arrow up or down, that will select an entire row at a time.

With both methods, which side of the text you start on doesn't matter. You can start at the end and go to the beginning or start at the beginning and go to the end. Just be sure to start at one end or the other. You cannot start in the middle

The text you've selected will then be highlighted in gray. Like the words "sample text" in this image:

This is sample text so you can see what I'm talking about.

If you need to select text that isn't touching you can do this by selecting your first section of text and then holding down the Ctrl key and selecting your second section of text using your mouse. (You can't arrow to the second section of text or you'll lose your already selected text.)

Dropdown Menu

If you right-click in a Word document, you will see what I'm going to refer to as a dropdown menu. (Sometimes it will actually drop upward if you're towards the bottom of the document.)

A dropdown menu provides you a list of choices to select from.

There are also dropdown menus available for some of the options listed under the tabs at the top of the screen.

For example, if you go to the Paragraph section of the Home tab, you will see arrows next to the options for bulleted lists, numbered lists, multi-level lists, line and paragraph spacing, shading, and borders.

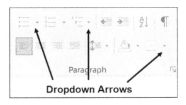

Dropdown Arrows

If you click on any of those arrows you'll see a list of additional choices.

Expansion Arrows

I don't know the official word for these, but you'll also notice at the bottom right corner of most of the sections in each tab that there are little arrows. If you hold your mouse over the arrow you will see a brief description of what clicking on the expansion arrow will do like below with Paragraph Settings.

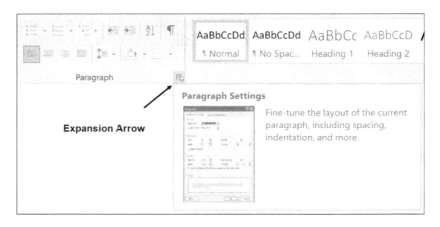

In general, clicking on that arrow will then open a dialogue box although sometimes a task pane will open instead.

Dialogue Box

Dialogue boxes, such as this one for Find and Replace, are pop-up boxes that cover specialized settings.

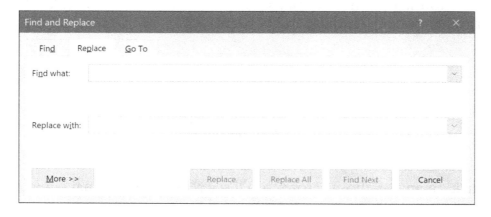

As just mentioned, if you click on an expansion arrow, it will often open a dialogue box that contains more choices than are visible in that section.

When you right-click in a Word document and choose Font, Paragraph, or Hyperlink from the dropdown menu that also opens a dialogue box

Some of the menu options will do so as well. For example, clicking on Replace in the Editing section of the Home tab will bring up the Find and Replace dialogue box. (As will using Ctrl + H, which is a control shortcut. We'll define those momentarily.)

Dialogue boxes often allow the most granular level of control over an option so if you can't find what you want in the menu section tabs at the top, try opening the relevant dialogue box.

Also, be aware that if you have more than one Word document open and open a dialogue box in one of those documents, you may not be able to move to the other documents you have open until you close the dialogue box.

Task Pane

Sometimes instead of opening a dialogue box, Excel will open what I refer to as a task pane. These are separate panes that appear to the right, left, or bottom of your main workspace. (As opposed to a dialogue box which generally appears as a separate item on top of your workspace.)

I believe the Navigation pane is open on the left-hand side by default for any new document for new users of Word. It will show headings if you use those in your document and is also the default location if you try to use Find in your document.

Task panes can be closed by clicking on the X in the top right corner. If you close the Navigation pane and want it back, Ctrl + F, which is for Find, will open it again.

Clicking on the expansion arrow for the Clipboard section of the Home tab also opens a task pane.

Scroll Bar

This is more useful in Excel than in Word, but on the right-hand side of the screen and sometimes at the bottom of the screen you may see a scroll bar which will allow you to see the rest of your document if it's too large or too long to be fully visible on the screen.

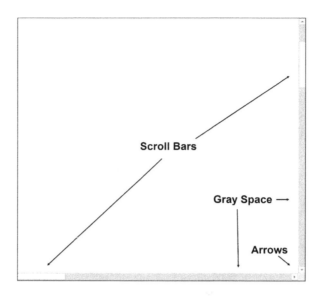

You can click in the gray space around the bar to move up or down a small amount. Or you can left-click on the bar, hold the left-click, and drag the bar to move through the document more quickly.

You can also use the arrows at the ends to move through your document.

The scroll bar isn't always visible in Word. If you don't see it, move your mouse over to the side of the screen and it should appear.

Also, by default you normally won't see a scroll bar at the bottom of the screen, but it is possible to see one, usually when you have your document or screen zoomed in.

Arrow

If I ever tell you to arrow to the left or right or up or down, that just means use your arrow keys. This will move your cursor to the left one space, to the right one space, up one line, or down one line. If you're at the end of a line and arrow to the right, it will take you to the beginning of the next line. If you're at the beginning of a line and arrow to the left, it will take you to the end of the last line.

Cursor

There are two possible meanings for cursor. One is the one I just used. In your Word document, you will see that there is a blinking line. This indicates where you are in the document. If you type text, each letter will appear where the cursor was at the time you typed it. The cursor will move (at least in the U.S. and I'd assume most European versions) to the right as you type. This version of the cursor should be visible at all times unless you have text selected.

The other type of cursor is the one that's tied to the movement of your mouse or trackpad. When you're typing, it will not be visible. But stop typing and move your mouse or trackpad, and you'll see it.

If the cursor is positioned over your text, it will look somewhat like a tall skinny capital I. If you move it up to the menu options or off to the sides, it becomes a white arrow. (Except for when you position it over any option under the tabs that can be typed in such as Font Size or Font where it will once again look like a skinny capital I.)

Usually I won't refer to your cursor, I'll just say, "click" or "select" or whatever action you need to take with it. Moving the cursor to that location will be implied.

I may also sometimes refer to this as moving your mouse or holding your mouse over something instead of moving your cursor or holding your cursor over an item.

Quick Access Toolbar

In the very top left corner of Word is something called the Quick Access Toolbar. By default it contains icons that let you save, undo, and redo. Bur you can customize your options for tasks that you use often by clicking on that arrow at the end and choosing from the dropdown menu it will bring up.

For example, I will usually customize mine to include inserting section breaks because those are listed on a different tab than the text formatting options I also need to be using at the same time. This saves me having to move back and forth between the two.

Control Shortcuts

What I refer to as control shortcuts are easy and quick ways to complete common tasks by using the Ctrl key paired with, generally, a letter.

I mentioned the Find control shortcut, Ctrl + F, above as well as the Replace shortcut, Ctrl + H. So, for example, by typing Ctrl and the letter H at the same time you can open the Replace dialogue box that allows you to replace text in your document with different text.

When I refer to a control shortcut, I write the letter as a capital letter, but you don't actually have to use the capitalized version of the letter. It just means hold down the control key and that letter at the same time.

There is a list of control shortcuts at the back of this book. It is not a comprehensive list, but I highly recommend that you memorize the ones that are there. They will save you a tremendous amount of time over the years.

Absolute Basics

Before we do anything else, there are a few absolute basics that we should cover.

Starting a New Word File

To start a brand new Word file, click on Word from your applications menu or, if you have one, the shortcut on your computer's taskbar. Either choice will bring up a welcome screen with a list of various options or templates, including the first one which is for a "Blank document". Ninety-nine percent of the time that's the one you'll want. To use it, left-click on the image.

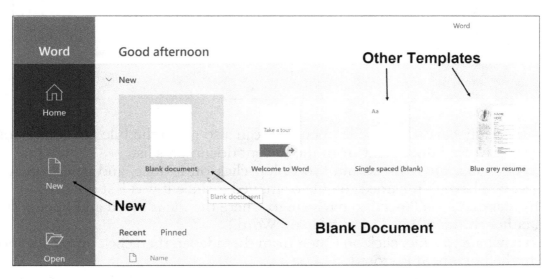

If you're already in Word and want to start a new Word file, go to the File tab and choose New from the left-hand menu. It will again show various choices. This time the Blank Document choice will be at the top and other templates will be shown below.

You can also the control shortcut Ctrl +N while in an existing document and a new blank document will immediately open.

Opening an Existing Word File

To open an existing Word file you can either go to the folder where the file is saved and double-click on the file name. Or, if the file is one you used recently, you can instead open Word and choose the file from the list of Recent documents. (If it's a file you've pinned even if it hasn't been used recently, you can still choose it from the list of Pinned documents.)

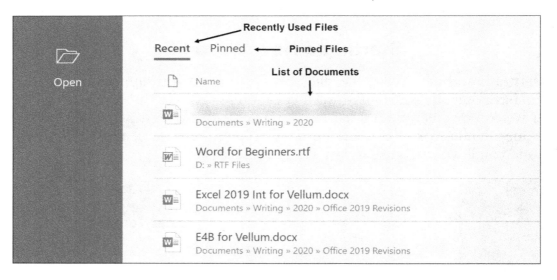

If you already have a Word file open, you can also go to the File tab and choose any recently used document from the Recent documents list.

To choose a file from within Word, left-click on it once, and it will open as long as you haven't renamed the file or moved it since it was last opened.

(In that case, you'll need to navigate to where the file is saved and open it that way, either through Word or outside of Word.)

To navigate to a file, click on Open from the sidebar, then click on the location where the document is stored.

If you use OneDrive click on that. I don't, so I click on Browse to open a standard Windows dialogue box. Mine defaults to the Documents folder on This PC. I can then navigate through my folders or shortcuts from there and click on the file I need.

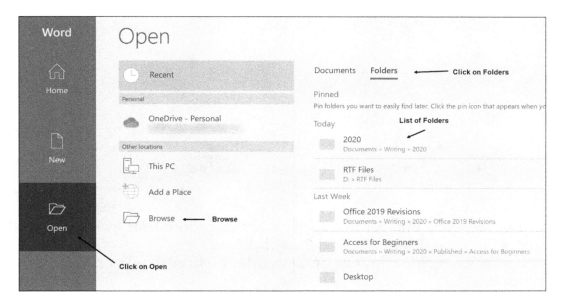

You can also click on Folders on the right-hand side to display a list of folders that contain files you've recently used. Click on one of the folder names to bring up a list of the files and folders that are in that folder.

It will show the files and folders within the Word workspace. Only documents that can be opened in Word will be listed.

Saving a Word File

If you want to keep the changes you made to a document, you need to save it. To do so quickly, you can use Ctrl + S or click on the small image of a floppy disk in the Quick Access Toolbar in the top left corner of the screen above File.

For a document you've already saved, that will overwrite the prior version of the document with the current version while keeping the file name, file type, and file location the same.

If you try to save a file that has never been saved before, Word will automatically default to the Save As option and open a Save This File dialogue box which asks for the file name you want to use and a location to save the file in.

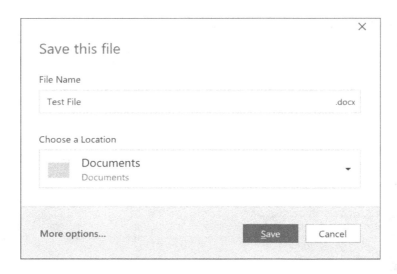

Type your file name into the box for File Name, choose your location from the Choose a Location dropdown, and then click Save.

The default file type with this option is .docx which should be fine for most purposes.

If you are working with someone who has a version of Word that dates prior to 2007, you'll need to save the file as a .doc file. To do so, click on the More Options choice at the bottom of the dialogue box.

This will take you to the Save As option on the File tab screen. From there you can double-click on a location to save your file and this will open a Save As dialogue box which lets you choose your file type as well.

Even for an existing document there will still be times when you need to use the Save As option to change the location of a file, the name of a file, or the file type.

(With respect to file type, I often need to save a .doc file as a .pdf file or a .docx file or to save a .docx file as a .doc file, for example.)

You can reach the Save As option while working with an existing file by clicking on the File tab and then the Save As option on the left-hand side.

From there double-click on your location and make whatever necessary changes you need to make in the dialogue box that opens. (If the location is not listed, you can get the dialogue box to open and then navigate to your preferred location using the left-hand side options.)

To rename a file, it's actually best to close the file and then go to where the file is currently saved and rename it that way rather than using the Save As option within Word.

This is because if you use Save As, Word will keep the original version of the file with the old name as well as create a version with the new name. That's great when you want version control, but not when you just wanted to rename your file and now can't remember which version is the most current one.

(This is a good opportunity to point out that using something like YYYYMMDD or V1, V2, etc. in your file names can really help with keeping version control. If I have a file named Great Report 20201220 and one named Great Report 20201101, I can easily tell which is the most current version. They will also sort in order if you use YYYYMMDD format for the dates in the file name and place the date in the exact same spot in the name each time.)

Renaming a Word File

As discussed above, you can use Save As to give an existing file a new name, but that approach will leave you with two versions of the file, one with the old name and one with the new name. If you just want to change the name of the existing file, close it and then navigate to where you've saved it.

Click on the file name once to select it, click on it a second time to highlight the name, and then type in the new name you want to use, replacing the old one.

If you rename the file this way outside of Word, there will only be one version of the file left, the one with the new name you wanted.

Just be aware that if you rename a file by navigating to where it's located and changing the name that you then won't be able to access the file from the Recent Workbooks listing under Open file, since that listing will still list the old name which no longer exists.

(This actually applies for any file that is moved, renamed, or in a location that is no longer available. If you look at that file listing above, my file Word for Beginners was in a location D: which was a removable thumb drive. I don't have that thumb drive attached to my computer at the moment, so if I tried to click on that file name right now I would see an error telling me that the directory name isn't valid. I personally run into this issue more with moved files than I do with renamed ones, but it's something to be aware of.)

Deleting a Word File

You can't delete a Word file from within Word. You need to close the file you want to delete and then navigate to where the file is stored and delete the file there without opening it. Once you've located the file, click on the file name. (Only enough to select it. Make sure you haven't double-clicked and highlighted the name which will delete the file name but not the file.) Next, choose Delete from the menu at the top of the screen, or right-click and choose Delete from the dropdown menu.

Closing a Word File

To close a Word file click on the X in the top right corner. You can also go to File and then choose Close which will keep Word open if that was your last Word file.

(You can also use Ctrl + W, but I never have. That also closes the file but leaves Word open.)

If no changes were made to the document since you saved it last, the document will just close.

If changes have been made, Word will ask you if you want to save those changes. Your choices are to Save, Don't Save, or Cancel. For a brand new document you need to provide a file name and choose a location. For an existing one, Word will assume the file name and location are going to stay the same.

If you cancel, the document remains open. If you save, it will overwrite the prior version of the document with any changes you've made. If you choose don't save, then the version of the document that remains will be the one that existed last time you saved. Or, in the case of a new document, that document will be lost.

I almost always default to saving any changes. If I'm in doubt about whether I'd be overwriting something important, I cancel and choose to Save As and save the current file as a later version of the document just in case (e.g., Great Book v2).

If right before you closed the document you copied an image or a large block of text, you may also see a dialogue box asking if you want to keep that image or text on the clipboard to paste elsewhere Usually the answer for me is no, but if you had planned on pasting that image or text somewhere else and hadn't yet done so, you can say to keep it on the clipboard.

Basic Tasks

At its most basic, adding text into a Word document is incredibly simple. Just open a new blank document and start typing. When you're done, save the document.

But you probably want to do more with your text than that.

We'll cover all the formatting, which is the majority of what you'll want to do, in the next section. First, I want to cover a few basic tasks in Word that will make your life easier as you enter your text and then edit it.

Undo

Undo lets you take the last thing (or few things) you did, and undo it. That means you don't have to be afraid to try something that you're not sure will work, because you can always reverse it.

To undo something, simply type Ctrl + Z. If you did a few things you didn't like you can keep typing Ctrl + Z until they're all gone.

Your other option is to use the undo arrow in the Quick Access Toolbar. It's the left-pointing arrow and will only be an option to click on when there's something that can be undone.

When there are multiple actions that can be undone the Quick Access Toolbar option will also include a dropdown arrow. You can click on it to see a full listing of what actions can be undone.

Keep in mind that Word undoes things in order. So if you highlighted text, bolded that text, and then underlined it and you want to undo the highlight, you'll have to undo the bolding and underline as well.

You can't pick and choose.

When there are multiple steps to undo the Quick Access Toolbar option is the better choice because you can simply choose the last item on the list that you wanted to undo and it as well as all of the actions that were taken after it will be undone.

Redo

If you take it too far and undo too much and want something back, then you can choose to redo. That's done by typing Ctrl + Y.

There is also a Redo option on the Quick Access Toolbar. It's the right-pointing arrow.

It works much like the Undo option since it's only available when there is something that can be redone, but it will only redo one action at a time. So in my example above where I could undo three actions at once, to put them back in place I had to do each one individually.

Delete

Another basic task you need to master is how to delete text. There are a few ways to do this. If you're trying to delete something that you just typed, use the backspace key to delete the letters one at a time.

You can also click into your text to place the cursor next to the text you want to delete and then use the backspace or delete keys depending on where the cursor is relative to the text you're trying to delete.

If your cursor is on the left-hand side of text, use the delete key. If it's on the right-hand side, use the backspace key. (And if you get it wrong, remember that you have Ctrl + Z to undo what you just did.)

If you want to delete a large chunk of text at one time, select the text first and then use the delete OR backspace key.

Select All

The other basic task that you should know about before we start talking formatting is how to select all of the text in your document.

Select All is very useful for applying a format to your entire document or for copying text from one document to another or another program.

I tend to write in the default font that Word uses and then change the font once I'm done, for example.

The easiest way to select all of your text is to use Ctrl + A. You can also go to the Editing section of the Home tab, click on the arrow next to Select, and choose Select All from the dropdown menu.

I have also added Select All as one of my Quick Access Toolbar options in the past.

If you ever choose all of the text in a document and then decide you didn't want to, just click somewhere in the document and the selection will go away. (You can also arrow up or down, but that will take you to the top or the bottom of the document and you may not want that.)

Copying, Cutting, and Pasting

Copy and Cut are similar. They're both a way to move text from one location to another. Copy leaves the text where it was and creates a copy of that text to move to the new location. Cut removes the text from where it was and puts the text on a "clipboard" (that's usually not visible to you) for movement to a new location.

Paste is how you tell Word where that new location is regardless of whether you copied or cut the text.

The first step in copying or cutting text is to select all of the text you want to move.

As discussed before, to select text you can left-click at one end of the text, hold down that left-click and move your mouse or trackpad until all of the text you want is highlighted. Or you can click at one end of the text and use the shift key and the arrow keys. Your selected text will be highlighted in gray.

Once your text is selected, to copy it type Ctrl + C or to cut it type Ctrl + X.

If you don't want to use the control shortcuts, you can also go to the Clipboard section of the Home tab and choose Copy or Cut from there. Or you can right-click and choose Copy or Cut from the dropdown menu.

I recommend using the control shortcuts, because it's the easiest and fastest option and doesn't require using your mouse or trackpad.

If you copy text, it remains visible in the location you copied it from. Behind the scenes Word has taken a copy of that text and placed it on a "clipboard" for use elsewhere.

If you cut text, the text is immediately removed from the document. It too is placed on a "clipboard" for use elsewhere. (This also means that cutting text, if you choose not to paste it elsewhere, deletes it.)

If you want to collect multiple selections of text to eventually paste elsewhere, click on the expansion arrow for the Clipboard section of the Home tab. This will open the clipboard. You can then select different sections of your document and copy or cut them and they should appear on the clipboard for your use.

(It looks like it should also work even if you don't have the clipboard open at the time you're copying or cutting multiple selections, but best practice would be to have it visible so you know that the items your are copying or cutting are being captured properly.) Here I've selected three snippets of text. Two were copied, one was cut, but there's no difference in how they appear on the clipboard.

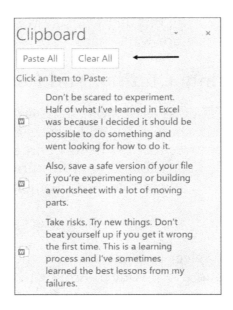

If you ever copy or cut items to your clipboard and decide you don't want them, just choose Clear All. Otherwise click on where you want to paste an individual item in your document and then click on the item in the clipboard to paste it.

The Paste All option will paste all of your copied or cut selections into that one location.

Items remain on the clipboard after they are pasted which means you can technically paste something into your document multiple times using the clipboard option.

If all you want to do is just copy or cut one thing and paste it one time, then using the paste control shortcut is going to be easier. To paste use Ctrl + V. So highlight your selection, copy (Ctrl + C) or cut (Ctrl +X) it, go to where you want to place it and click into the document, use Ctrl + V to paste it, and you're done.

Rather than use Ctrl + V to paste you can also go to the Clipboard section of the Home tab and click on Paste from there or right-click in your document and choose one of the Paste options from the dropdown menu.

The reason to use one of those options instead of just Ctrl + V is because it gives you control over the formatting of the text when you paste it, so let's talk about those options now.

Paste Options

If you use Ctrl + V to paste text, you'll be pasting not only the text you copied or cut, but its formatting as well. Usually, that's fine and you'll probably be able to use Ctrl + V ninety-five percent of the time.

(Even if you ultimately don't want to keep the formatting, there's a trick I'll show you later—using the Format Painter—that you can use to quickly correct formatting after you paste the text into its new location. All the Format Painter requires is that you have some text that's already formatted the way you want so you can copy its formatting.)

But in case you do want control over how you paste in your text, that's where the Paste Options can be used. There are four paste options: Keep Source Formatting, Merge Formatting, Picture, and Keep Text Only.

As you can see here, when you hold your cursor over each option it will tell you which option that one is. I have my cursor over the first option which is Keep Source Formatting and that description is shown directly below the option as I hold my cursor there.

The best way to figure out what each of these options does is to just experiment with them. That's what I've done below.

I took the word TEST and I formatted it in a larger font, a different font, bolded it, colored the text red, and highlighted the text in yellow. (You may not see all of that in print, but I can describe it for you.) I then copied that text and pasted it into each of my sample sentences using the different paste methods above.

The first paste option was just using Ctrl + V and that pasted the text in with all of the formatting I'd applied still in place.

The second option, Keep Formatting, also kept everything. The third option, Merge Formatting, lost the different font size, different font, font color, and highlight. But it kept the bolding.

The fourth option, Picture, actually pasted the copied text in as a picture in a picture box.

And the final option, Keep Text Only stripped way all of the formatting I'd applied, including the bolding.

Interesting, but my recommendation is to stick to Ctrl + V and use the Format Painter when and if needed.

Okay. On to text formatting. If you remember anything from what we just walked through, remember this:

Ctrl + C to copy.

Ctrl + X to cut.

Ctrl + V to paste.

Text Formatting

Now that you know how to create a file, enter the text you want, and save your work, it's time to actually format that text. Let's start with font.

Fonts

Choosing a Font – General Thoughts

Word 2019 uses Calibri font as the default, but there are hundreds of fonts you can choose from and the font you use will govern the general appearance of the text in your document. Here is a sample of a few of those choices written in each font:

Sans-Serif Font Examples:

Calibri

Arial

Gill Sans MT

Serif Font Examples:

Times New Roman

Garamond

Palatino Linotype

The first three samples are sans-serif fonts. (That just means they don't have little feet at the bottom of the letters.) The second three samples are serif fonts. (They do have those little feet at the bottom of each letter.)

All of these fonts are the same size, but you can see that the different fonts have a different appearance and take up different amounts of space on the page. Arial is darker and taller than Calibri, for example.

Many corporations have a standard font they want you to use to be consistent with their brand and places like literary magazines will often specify which font to use for submitting stories. If that doesn't happen I'd suggest using a serifed font like Garamond or Times New Roman for main body text since a serifed font is supposed to be easier to read. Sans-serif fonts are good for headers or titles or for display text.

Also, unless you're working on a creative project, I'd recommend that you don't get too fancy with your fonts. Certain fonts, like Comic Sans, are so well-known for misuse that they are an immediate indicator that someone doesn't know design or isn't "professional."

The six fonts listed above are ones I'd generally consider safe.

Remember, at the end of the day, the goal is to communicate effectively, which means that a font like Algerian as main body text is not a good idea because readers will focus on the font and not the words.

Font Selection

Okay. So how do you change the font used in your document?

There are a few options.

But before we discuss those, let me point out that if you already know you want to use a different font, it's easier to change the font before you start typing. Once you do so, any new text will be in the new font.

Otherwise you'll need to select all of the text you want to change and then choose your font, which can be tricky if you're using different fonts for your headers and main body text

(A situation like that's also a good time to use Styles which is an intermediate-level topic covered in *Word 2019 Intermediate*.)

The first way to change the font is through the Font section of the Home tab. Click on the arrow to the right of the current font and choose a new one from the dropdown menu.

The first section of the dropdown menu lists the fonts for the theme you're using. Usually that'll be the defaults for Word, in this case, Calibri and Calibri Light.

Next you'll see Recently Used Fonts. (Most of the time there will only be one or two fonts there, but I had used a number recently.)

Finally, below those sections will be an alphabetical listing of all available fonts. If you know the font you want, you can start typing in its name rather than scroll through the entire list. Otherwise, use the scroll bar on the right-hand side or the up and down arrows to move through the list.

Each font is written using that font to give you an idea what it will look like. See for example the difference between Algerian and Garamond above.

The next way to change your font is to right-click and choose Font from the dropdown menu. This will bring up the Font dialogue box. In the top left corner you can choose the font you want.

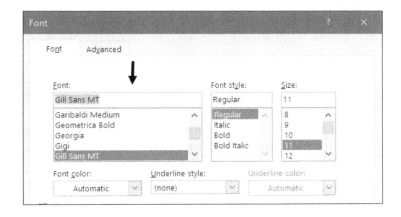

There's a third option for changing the font, something I'm going to call the mini formatting menu. If you highlight your text it will appear on the screen when you let up on the left-click.

It will also appear above or below the dropdown menu if you right-click in your Word document.

As you can see, one of the options that you can change in the mini formatting menu is the font. In the example above, the current font is Arial, but I could click on the arrow on the right-hand side and change that. The dropdown menu looks the exact same as the one from the Font section of the Home tab we saw above.

Regardless of where you choose to change the font, if the font listing is blank that's because you have selected text that contains more than one font.

Font Size

Font size dictates how large the text will be. Here are some examples of different font sizes in Garamond font:

8 point 12 point 16 point

As you can see, the larger the font size, the larger the text for that specific font. Most documents are written in a ten, eleven, or twelve point font size. Often footnotes or endnotes will use eight or nine point size. Chapter headings or title pages will use the larger font sizes.

Whatever font size you do use, try to be consistent between different sections of your document. So all main body text should use just one font size. Same for chapter or section headings.

Changing the font size works much the same way as changing the font. You have the same three options: You can go to the Font section of the Home tab, bring up the mini formatting menu by right-clicking or selecting your text, or bring up the Font dialogue box by right-clicking and choosing Font from the dropdown menu.

If you want to change existing text, you need to select the text first. Otherwise, change the font size before you start typing.

For all three options the current font size is listed to the right of the current font name in the Font section of the Home tab.

If you use the Home tab or the mini formatting menu there is a dropdown list of font sizes to choose from that you can see by clicking on the arrow next to the current font size. In the Font dialogue box that list of choices is already visible in a box under the current value.

If the font size you want isn't one of the choices listed you can type in the value you want instead by clicking into the box that shows the current font size and changing that number to the size you want just like you would with text in the main document.

With the Home tab and the mini formatting menu you can also increase your font size one listed value at a time by using the increase and decrease font options directly to the right of the font size.

These are depicted as the letter A with a small arrow above it that points either upward or downward. The one on the left with the arrow that points upward will increase the font size. The one on the right with the arrow that points downward will decrease the font size.

The values available with that option are the ones in the font size dropdown menu, so you can increase from 14 point to 16 point but not to 15 point using this option.

Font Color

Changing your font color works the same as changing your font or font size. Select the text you want to change and then either go to the Font section of the Home tab, pull up the mini formatting menu, or right-click and choose Font from the dropdown menu to bring up the Font dialogue box.

This time you want to click on the arrow next to the A with the solid colored line under it in the bottom right corner of the Font section:

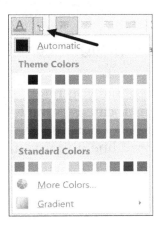

That line is red by default but will change as you use the tool and will stay the mostly recently selected color until you close the document.

Clicking on the dropdown arrow will give you a dropdown menu with seventy different colors to choose from. Simply click on the color you want and it will change your selected text to that color.

If those seventy choices are not enough, you can click on More Colors at the bottom of the dropdown box to bring up the Colors dialogue box where you can choose from even more colors on the Standard tab or specify a color in the Custom tab using RGB or HSL values.

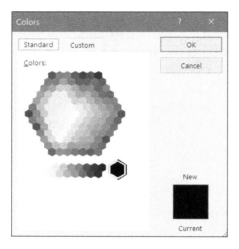

Once you select a font color any new text will be in that color. To go back to the default color choose Automatic from the dropdown menu.

Other Text Formatting

Highlight Text

You can also highlight text much like you might do with a highlighter using the Text Highlighter option which is located to the left of the Font Color option in the Font section of the Home tab or in the mini formatting menu. It has the letters ab and a pen with a colored line underneath.

By default the line is bright yellow but that changes as the tool is used.

To apply highlighting, select the text you want to highlight, and then either click on that option to highlight the text in the currently-displayed color or click on the dropdown arrow and choose from one of the fifteen color choices shown there.

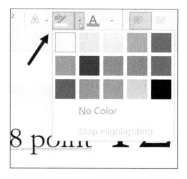

To remove a highlight select the highlighted text, go to the highlight dropdown, and choose the No Color option. Once used, a highlight will *not* be applied to new text.

Bold Text

This is one you will probably use often. At least I do. As you can see with the headers in this chapter.

The easiest way to bold text is to use Ctrl + B.

You can use it before you start typing the text you want to bold or on a selection of text that you've chosen.

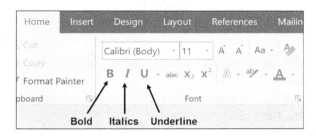

If you don't want to use the control keys, you can also go to the Font Section of the Home tab and click on the B on the left-hand side.

The final option is to select your text, right-click, choose Font from the dropdown menu, and then choose Bold in the Font Style section of the Font dialogue box.

(If you want to both bold and italicize text, you would choose Bold Italic.)

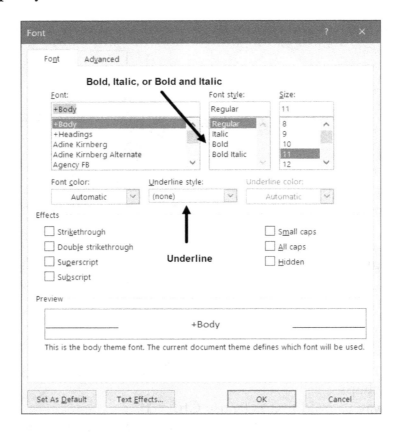

Italicize Text

To place text into italics—that means to have it sloped to the side like the subsection headers in this section for Italicize Text and Underline Text—the easiest way is to use Ctrl + I.

It works the exact same way as bolding text. You can do it before you type the letters or select the text and then use it.

Another option is to click on the slanted capital I in the Font section of the Home tab.

Or if you use the Font dialogue box select Italic under Font Styles. Or Bold Italic to have both italicized and bolded text.

Underline Text

Underlining text works much the same way as bolding or italicizing text.

The simplest way is to use Ctrl + U.

Or in the Font section of the Home tab you can click on the underlined U in the bottom row of the Font section.

There is also an Underline Style dropdown in the Font dialogue box.

Underline is different from italics and bold, however, because there are multiple underline options to choose from.

Using Ctrl + U will provide a single line underline of your text. So will just clicking on the U in the Font section of the Home tab. But if you click on the arrow next to the U in the Font section, you will see seven additional underline options to choose from including dotted and wavy lines.

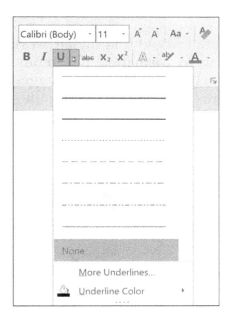

Choosing More Underlines at the bottom of that list of options will open the Font dialogue box where you have a total of sixteen underline styles to choose from.

Remove Bolding, Underlining, or Italics

If you have bolded, underlined, or italicized text and you want to remove that formatting, you can simply select the text and use the command in question to remove that formatting.

So Ctrl + B, I, or U. Or you can click on the letter in the Font section of the Home tab or go to the Font dialogue box and remove the formatting from there.

If you select text that is partially formatted one way and partially formatted another—so say half of it is bolded and half is not—you will need to use the command twice. The first time will apply the formatting to all of the selected text, the second time will remove it from all of the selected text.

Also, with specialty underlining using Ctrl + U will initially revert the type of underlining to the basic single underline. To remove the underline altogether, you'll need to use Ctrl + U a second time.

Copy Formatting

Now for a text formatting trick that has saved me more times than I can count, the Format Painter.

Often in my corporate life I would find myself working on a group document where different sections were formatted differently. Usually it was a subtle difference such as the space between lines in a paragraph. Rather than guess and poke around trying to figure out what was causing the difference, I would use the Format Painter to copy the formatting from a "good" section to the rest of the document.

The Format Painter is located in the Clipboard section of the Home tab.

You can also access it in the mini formatting menu.

What it does is it takes all of the formatting from your selected text and applies it to the text you choose. This means color, font, font size, paragraph spacing, etc. All of it changes.

To use it, select the text with the formatting you want to copy (generally I select a whole paragraph or more), then click on Format Painter, then select the text you want to transfer the formatting to.

You need to use the mouse or trackpad to select the text you want to transfer your formatting to because using the arrow keys or the arrow and shift keys won't work

You'll know that the format painter is ready to transfer the format when you see a little paintbrush next to your cursor as you hover over your document. Format Painter in the Home tab will also be highlighted gray.

To turn it off without using it, use Esc.

If you double-click on the Format Painter it will remain available for use on multiple selections until you hit Esc or start typing in your document or click on it again.

A few more tips:

The format painter can be unreliable if there are different formats in the sample you're taking the formatting from. For example, if part of the text is red and part of the text is bolded and I format sweep from that sample to new text, only the formatting of the first letter in the sample will transfer.

Another issue worth mentioning. Sometimes with paragraph or numbered list formatting, I have to select the paragraph from the bottom instead of from the top in order to get the format painter to carry over the paragraph formatting I want. (This is also why I sometimes select multiple paragraphs.)

It's also possible to sweep formatting that's in one document to another document.

Last but not least, when you copy formatting over, *all* of the formatting in your target text will be removed. This can be an issue if you've used italics or bolding within a paragraph, for example.

That means you may have to go back and put the bold and italic formatting in manually, but sometimes Format Painter is the only way to get paragraphs formatted the same even when they appear to have the exact same settings in place.

Okay, then. On now to a discussion of paragraph formatting.

Paragraph Formatting

What we just discussed was basic text formatting. Now it's time to cover paragraph formatting which includes text alignment, line spacing, the space between paragraphs, indents, etc.

Here we're just going to discuss how to change the formatting of a specific paragraph but once you're comfortable enough in Word, I'd advise that you also learn to use Styles which will let you format one paragraph the way you want it, create a style from that paragraph, and then apply that Style to all other paragraphs that you want to have the same formatting. (It's covered in *Word 2019 Intermediate* or you can learn about it through Word's help function.)

Alright then. Let's talk about how to format a paragraph one element at a time.

Paragraphs

Alignment

There are four choices for paragraph alignment. Left, Center, Right, and Justified. The easiest way to choose your paragraph formatting option is via the Paragraph section of the Home tab. All four options are shown in the bottom row and are formatted to show the alignment they represent.

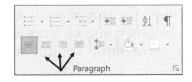

In the image below I've taken the same three-line paragraph and applied each alignment style to it to show the difference between all four using real paragraphs of text:

This paragraph is **left-aligned**. And now I need to write enough additional text so that you can see what happens when a paragraph falls across multiple lines of text since that can be one of the most significant differences between the choices.

This paragraph is **center-aligned**. And now I need to write enough additional text so that you can see what happens when a paragraph falls across multiple lines of text since that can be one of the most significant differences between the choices.

This paragraph is **right-aligned**. And now I need to write enough additional text so that you can see what happens when a paragraph falls across multiple lines of text since that can be one of the most significant differences between the choices.

This paragraph is **justified**. And now I need to write enough additional text so that you can see what happens when a paragraph falls across multiple lines of text since that can be one of the most significant differences between the choices.

Left-aligned, the first example, is how you'll often see text in documents. The text of each line is lined up along the left-hand side of the page and allowed to end in a jagged line on the right-hand side of the page.

Justified, the last example, is the other common way for text to be presented. Text is still aligned along the left-hand side, but instead of leaving the right-hand side ragged, Word adjusts the spacing between words so that all lines are also aligned along the right-hand side. (That's how the paragraphs in the print version of this book are formatted.)

Centered, the second example, is rarely used for full paragraphs of text like above, but is often used for section headers or titles or quotes. When text is centered the ends of each line are equally distant from the center of the line. You can end up with jagged left and right margins as a result and a final line, like above, may be substantially away from the edges.

Right-aligned, the third example above, is rare for paragraphs, at least in the U.S. and other countries where text goes from left to right. It aligns each line of text along the right-hand side and leaves the left-hand side ragged.

I have seen right-alignment used for text in side margins of non-fiction books and would expect to see it used for languages that read right to left.

So that's the difference between the choices. Like I said, I use Styles or the Home tab to change my paragraph alignment, but there are also control shortcuts that you can use. Ctrl + L will left-align, Ctrl + E will center your text,

Ctrl + R will right-align, and Ctrl + J will justify it. The only one I use enough to have memorized is Ctrl + E.

The third way to change your paragraph alignment is to select your text, right-click, and choose Paragraph from the dropdown menu to bring up the Paragraph dialogue box. The first option within that box is a dropdown where you can choose the alignment type you want. It has the exact same four formatting types that are available in the Home tab.

Spacing of a Single Paragraph

If you've ever attended school in the United States, you've probably been told at some point to submit a five-page paper that's double-spaced with one inch margins. Or if you've ever submitted a short story you were told to use a specific line spacing. In Word this is referred to as Line Spacing. So how do you do it?

As with the other formatting options, you can either do this before you start typing or by selecting the paragraphs you want to change after they've been entered into the document.

Once you're ready, go to the Paragraph section of the Home tab and locate the Line and Paragraph Spacing option. It's to the right of the paragraph alignment options and looks like five lines of text with two big blue up and down arrows on the left-hand side.

Click on the small black arrow to the right of the image to bring up the dropdown menu.

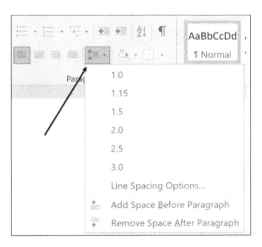

You have a choice of single-spaced (1.0) double-spaced (2.0), or triple-spaced (3.0) as well as 1.15, 1.5, and 2.5 spacing.

Below are examples of single, double, and triple-spaced paragraphs, Note how the amount of space between each row of text increases as you move from single-spaced up to triple-spaced:

This is a sample paragraph to show you the difference between line spacing. This is a **single-spaced** (1.0) paragraph. I'm going to keep typing so there are three lines of text to help you see the difference.

This is a sample paragraph to show you the difference between line spacing. This

is a **double-spaced** (2.0) paragraph. I'm going to keep typing so there are three

lines of text to help you see the difference.

This is a sample paragraph to show you the difference between line spacing. This

is a **triple-spaced** (1.0) paragraph. I'm going to keep typing so there are three lines

of text to help you see the difference.

If you want a different spacing than one of the dropdown options, then click on Line Spacing Options at the bottom of the list to bring up the Paragraph dialogue box.

You can go straight to the Paragraph dialogue box (shown in the next section) by right-clicking and choosing Paragraph from the dropdown menu. This setting is shown under the heading Line Spacing in the third section of the dialogue box which is labeled Spacing. It is on the right-hand side.

The dropdown menu gives you the choice of Single, 1.5, and Double as well as At Least, Exactly, and Multiple. Multiple lets you enter any value (such as 3 for triple-spacing). At Least and Exactly base the line spacing off of the number of points. So if you have 12 pt text, you can make the line spacing Exactly 12 point as well.

(This is often where I find that in corporate settings someone has tweaked the line spacing on a paragraph so that it doesn't match the rest of the paragraphs in the document. I usually fix it with the Format Painter, but if you don't want to use that, this is another setting to check.)

Okay. On to the spacing between paragraphs.

Spacing Between Paragraphs

There are basically two accepted ways to format paragraphs for most writing. One is what you see in the print version of this book where there are paragraphs without spacing between them but each new paragraph in a section after the first is indented to show that a new paragraph has begun. (Sometimes the first paragraph will also be indented.)

The second option is to start every paragraph on the left-hand side, but to add space between the lines to separate the paragraphs.

By default Word will add spacing between your paragraphs, but you can change the settings so that that does not happen or you can adjust the amount of space that Word adds.

Also, for items like titles or section headers (like you see on this page), it is better to add spacing to separate your text rather than use an extra blank line, because as your document adjusts to new text that extra line here or there can impact the appearance of the document. You may suddenly end up with a blank line on the top of the page that you never wanted there, for example.

And, please, for the love of everything, do not add lines between paragraphs by using enter unless the document is just for you or will only be seen by someone else in a printed format. That's about as bad as using the tab key to indent your paragraphs. (Don't do that either. Use indenting which we'll talk about next.)

Okay, so where do you go to adjust the spacing between your paragraphs? If all you want to do is remove any existing spacing, you can do that in the same dropdown we looked at above. It's the Remove Space After Paragraph option.

If someone has already removed the space after a paragraph and all you want to do is add it back in, you can also use that dropdown and select Add Space After Paragraph. (It's not listed above because there was already a space for the paragraph I was working with, but if your paragraph does not have a space after it, that will be an option you can choose.)

Be careful with the dropdown because it also, as you can see above, can have an Add Space Before Paragraph option. That will put the space above your paragraph as opposed to below it.

For this one, though, I tend to work in the Paragraph dialogue box which you can access by choosing Line Spacing Options in the dropdown or by right-clicking and choosing Paragraph from the dropdown menu in the main workspace:

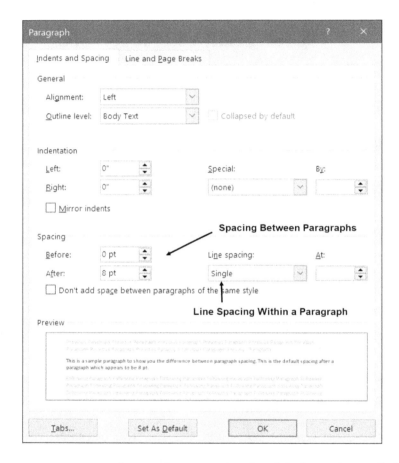

The spacing between paragraphs options are in the third section of the dialogue box, which is labeled Spacing, and on the left-hand side. There is a box for Before and one for After.

If you set your paragraphs to have spacing both before and after, the space between two paragraphs will be the higher of those two values not the combination of them. (So if you say 12 point before and 6 point after, the spacing between them will be 12 point not 18 point.)

If you just wanted spacing at the top of a section of paragraphs or at the bottom of a section of paragraphs but not between them, you can click the box to say don't add spacing to paragraphs of the same style Another option is to just add paragraph spacing to that top-most or bottom-most paragraph (although if you're working with Styles I wouldn't recommend that because you can accidentally override it.)

Below are examples of different paragraph spacing after paragraphs. I have no spacing, the default space that you get from the dropdown which is 8 pt, and 14 pt spacing just to show a visual difference. Because this is a screenshot they may not in fact be 8 and 14 pt spaces, but you can see the relative difference in appearance between each one.

> This is a sample paragraph to show you the difference between paragraph spacing. There is **no spacing** after this paragraph.
> This is a sample paragraph to show you the difference between paragraph spacing. This is the **default spacing** after a paragraph which appears to be 8 pt.
>
> This is another sample paragraph to show you the difference between paragraph spacing. This time I'm going to put a **14 pt space** after this paragraph.
>
> And this is final paragraph so you can see the spacing above.

Usually if I set a spacing I don't go above the font point size. The above font was 11 point in the document I was using, so in that case my spacing would normally be no more than 11 pt. (If I was writing a large-print document that might not be the case, so know your audience and the standards for that audience.)

Okay. So that was spacing within paragraphs and then spacing between paragraphs. As I mentioned above, if you have no spacing between paragraphs, the standard for indicating a new paragraphs is to add an indent to the first line of each new paragraph. Let's discuss how to do that now.

Indenting

Word provides two indenting options in the Paragraph section of the Home tab, but neither one will not give the first-line indent we need. They move the entire paragraph in or out.

For indenting a single line you need to use the Paragraph dialogue box which can be opened by right-clicking within your document and choosing Paragraph from the dropdown menu.

The second section of the dialogue box is labeled Indentation and covers whole paragraph and single line indents.

The whole paragraph indent options are on the left-hand side. The single-line or hanging indent option (which indents all but the first line of a paragraph) options are on the right-hand side.

Here I have settings for a paragraph with a first line indent:

And here are examples of the various indenting choices:

> This is a paragraph with **no indentation**. I am now going to make it long enough so that you can see what happens with the second line as well.
>
> This is a paragraph with a **left indent of .2"**. I am now going to make it long enough so that you can see what happens with the second line.
>
> This is a paragraph with a **right indent of .2"**. I am now going to make it long enough so that you can see what happens with the second line.
>
> This is a paragraph where the **first line has an indent of .2"** but the rest of the paragraph has no indent added.
>
> This is a paragraph where the indent is a **hanging indent of .2"** but the rest of the paragraph has no indent added.

The first example above has no paragraph indent.

The second and third show indents from the left and right-hand sides, respectively. Each is indented by .2" and you can see that on the side where it's indented it either starts or ends earlier than the non-indented paragraph.

(I formatted the paragraphs as Justified so that they'd fit the entire line and make that difference more obvious.)

The fourth example has the first line indented, but the remaining lines would not be. So you can see that "added" on the second line is as far left as the unindented paragraph at the top.

The final example is of a hanging indent where the first line is not indented, but the second and any subsequent lines would be.

To indent an entire paragraph, change the value for Left or Right on the left-hand side of the Indentation section.

To indent just the first line of a paragraph, choose First Line from the dropdown menu under Special on the right-hand side of the Indentation section and then specify by how much in the By box.

To create a hanging indent, choose Hanging from the Special dropdown and then specify the amount in the By box.

Remember to either do this in advance or to select the existing paragraphs you want to change before you start making your changes.

As I mentioned above, there are increase and decrease indent options in the Paragraph section of the Home tab. They're on the top row and show a series of lines with blue arrows pointing either to the left (to decrease an indent) or the right (to increase an indent).

They allow you to increase or decrease the indent for a paragraph or an entire selection of text from the left-hand side.

In my version of Word it indents by .5" the first time, then to a 1" indent the second time, and then to a 1.5" indent the third time.

If there are other indented paragraphs in the document, such as the ones I added before that had a .2" indent, then it will indent to those points as well.

When you decrease the indent it should follow the same stopping points on the way back to zero.

I will often use these quick indent options when dealing with a bulleted or numbered list that I want to visually separate from the main text of my document.

Lists

Bulleted

A bulleted list is just what it sounds like, a list of items where each line starts with some sort of marker or bullet on the left-hand side. The most common bullet choice is probably a small dark black circle that's filled in, but Word has additional options you can choose from such as an open circle, a filled-in square, and a checkmark. (See image below.)

You can either start a bulleted list before you have your items ready or you can take a list of items, highlight them, and then apply a bulleted list.

With either option, the way to do this is to go to the Paragraph section of the Home tab and click on the arrow next to the bulleted list option to bring up a dropdown menu where you can select the type of bullet you want.

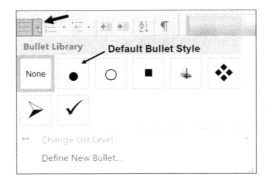

If you simply click on the image of the bulleted list instead of using the dropdown menu, your bullet will be a solid black circle.

Here are samples of each of the bullet choices shown above. (I had to create this by going into each line and choosing a different bullet type for that line. The default with bulleted lists is that once you choose a bullet that will be the bullet used for every line.)

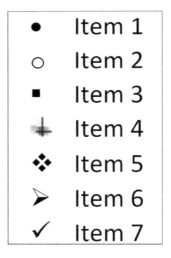

When you choose to insert a bulleted list, if you don't have any text selected already then a single bullet will appear on the page where your cursor was, waiting for you to type in your first entry.

If you do have items selected, each paragraph will be indented and the bullet type you chose will be added at the beginning of each of the paragraphs.

The mini formatting menu also has the bulleted list option available in the middle of the bottom row, so that's another option for applying or removing a bulleted list.

Once you've started a bulleted list each time you hit enter at the end of the text for a bulleted entry a new bullet will appear on the next line for you to add your next item.

Hit enter twice to return to normal paragraph indenting with no bullet. If you add a new bulleted list and then don't type any text before you hit enter again that will also revert back to no bullet.

(The double enter trick works for the first level of bullets. If you have a list with multiple levels of bullets, which we're about to cover, then you will need to hit enter until Word works its way through the levels of bullets and back to a blank option.)

You can create a bulleted list with multiple levels by using the Tab key to indent any line you want to the next level. Like so:

Here I've created three levels of indented text. I started with my first bullet and typed my text, then hit enter after Level 1. Next I used the tab to move that solid bullet in one level and create a second-level bullet. I then typed my text for that level and hit enter. And then repeated the process of tab, type, enter to create the other levels.

By default, when you hit enter from an existing line of a bulleted list the next line will be indented at that same level and will use the bullet mark for that level of indent.

To decrease an indent one level you can use Shift- + Tab.

When using Tab or Shift + Tab, if that line already has text in it be sure to place your cursor before any text. In the examples above, that would mean place it to the left of the first L in Level.

When you create a multi-level bulleted list, Word assigns a different bullet type for each indented level.

From what I can tell it uses the open circle for the first indented bullet, the black square for the second one, and then the black circle for the third one regardless of which option you chose for your first bullet. (See above.)

It then starts over again with the open circle for the next-level indent.

To change the bullet style for any level in your list, click on that line and go to the bulleted list options and choose a new bullet type.

That will apply that new bullet type to all lines in your list that are indented at that level. So, for example, all second-level indents will have the same bullet type and if you change that type for one line it will change it for *all* second-level indents in your list even if they are not listed together.

To remove bullets from a list, select the list, and then click on the bulleted list option in the Home tab or mini formatting menu. Your bullets will be removed, but the text will remain indented.

Another option for removing a bullet is to go to the beginning of the text for that line and backspace. Once will remove the bullet but keep the text where it is. Twice will move the text to the beginning of the line.

(You can also use the Format Painter to apply bullets to a list of entries or to remove them.)

With bulleted lists, Word will automatically indent your bullet and text when it adds the bullet for the first level. If you don't want that, you can use the Decrease Indent option to move the bullet back to the left-hand side of the page but keep the bullets.

If you decrease the indent for the first level of a multi-level bulleted list, this moves all levels back one indent.

The same works for increasing the indent using the Home tab option. If you increase the indent for the first level, it will increase the indent for all levels.

(For levels below that first level using Decrease Indent or Increase Indent just moves that specific line forward or backward one indent.)

You can also use the Paragraph dialogue box to have more control over how much each line is indented and whether each bulleted line should be treated as a hanging paragraph or not.

Another option you can use for indenting is the Adjust List Indents option from the dropdown menu on the main workspace. That will bring up the Adjust List Indents dialogue box.

This dialogue box allows you to choose the indent amount for the bullet. (It also is available for numbered lists, which we'll talk about next.)

The first choice is how much to indent the bullet or number.

The second choice is how much to indent the associated text.

The third choice is what type of separator to use between the bullet or number and the text. The default is a tab but you can also choose to use a space or nothing.

The choices you make here are probably more finicky for numbered lists than they are for bulleted lists since the bullet size remains constant no matter how many entries you have in your list. With numbered lists you have to move from 1 through 9 to 10 to 99 and then to 100 on which requires different amounts of space so each change can create a difference in the appearance of the list.

One more thing to note and then we'll move on to numbered lists.

I often will use the Paragraph dialogue box to add extra line spacing between bulleted list entries since sometimes I think entries in a list look better with a little more spacing between them than is used in a normal paragraph.

Numbered

A numbered list is similar to a bulleted list except the entries are either labeled with numbers or letters. If you've ever had to provide an outline of a paper for school, I'm sure you've run across a numbered list before.

One easy way to create a numbered list is to simply type the first number you want to use, the separator mark you want, and then a space.

So, for example, if I type a capital A and then a period and then a space that will give me the first entry in a numbered list that uses A, B, C, D, etc.

When I do that, Word automatically indents that text and turns it into the first entry in a numbered list so that when I type in my text and then hit enter the next line will be "numbered" in sequence and indented as well.

(If Word ever does that to you and you don't want it to indent and start creating a list, just use Ctrl + X to Undo. You can also click on the little AutoCorrect dropdown that appears to the left-hand side of the entry and choose to undo from there.)

The other option, especially if you already have your text entered and just need to convert it to a numbered list, is to select the lines you want to number, go to the Paragraph section of the Home tab, click on the arrow next to the Numbering option, and choose the numbered list option you want from there.

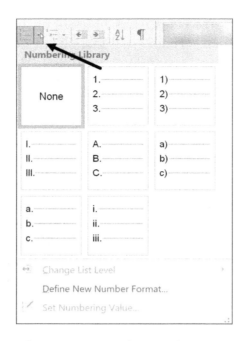

As you can see, you have the option to choose between lists that use

1, 2, 3

i, ii, iii

I, II, III

A, B, C

a, b, c

and then between using a period (.) or a paren( )) as the separator.

For a basic list, that should be all you really need. The default numbering choice if you just click on the image instead of using the dropdown is 1, 2, 3 separated with a period.

(In addition to the Home tab, the mini formatting menu also has the numbered list option.)

As with bulleted lists, you can create a multi-level list by using the tab key to indent a line or paragraph in your numbered list, but there appears to be that same pre-defined order for what will be used for each of the indented levels.

For the first indent Word uses the lower-case letters (a, b, c). For the second indent it uses lower-case Roman numerals (i, ii, iii). For the third indent it uses regular numbers (1, 2, 3). And then it cycles through again starting with the fourth-level indent. Like so:

```
1.  Level 1
        a.  Level 2
                i.  Level 3
                        1.  Level 4
                                a.  Level 5
```

This generally results in a multi-level list that doesn't fit what I was taught in school which was I, A, 1, a, i for the numbering order for different levels.

To create a list with customized numbering in each level, you'd need to use the Multilevel List option which we are not covering here because it has given me more problems over the years than probably anything else I've ever worked with in Word.

(It's the option to the right of the number list option in the Paragraph section if you want to experiment with it and I do reluctantly cover it in *Word 2019 Intermediate*.)

For now, back to basic numbered lists.

If you had a numbered list earlier in your document and want that numbering to continue with additional numbered items later in your document, you can do that. Likewise if Word continued the numbering and you didn't want it to, you can change the settings to restart the numbering.

In either case, create your numbered list and then right-click on the number for the line you want to change.

Depending on what else is in your document and which entry you click on, you will see different options in the dropdown menu.

Restart at 1 or Restart at A will change the number of the entry to 1 or A or whatever the first value would be for that numbering type. All you have to do is click on this one for it to be applied.

Continue Numbering is also applied immediately. Click on it to continue the numbering from the last time that numbering type was used. So if you have a list in your document that has the "numbers" A, B, C and another list that has numbering of 1 and 2 and the numbering style on your current line is the A, B, C style then when you choose to continue numbering your next entry will be D even if the 1 and 2 values are closer to that line in the document.

(If it sounds confusing, just play around with it in Word and you'll see what I'm talking about.)

The final option you'll see is Set Numbering Value which will bring up the Set Numbering Value dialogue box when you choose it.

This gives you the most control over what happens with your list numbering. You can restart the list, continue numbering, continue numbering with skipped numbers, or start numbering at any value you want.

If you do set the numbering at a random value, just be aware that your choices are based upon the list type for that line. So if it's a level that's numbered with Roman numerals then you'd have to use X for 10, you couldn't type in 10.

Be a little careful with all of this because a change to the numbering style of one entry will change all other linked lines which is great when that's what you want but can be dangerous if you're working with a very large document and don't realize that the list on page fifty is somehow tied into the list on page ten.

Always if you're working with numbered lists be sure to go back through your entire document at the end to make sure that a change you made towards the end of the document didn't change something at the beginning of the document.

(This actually goes for page or section breaks as well. Best practice is to always do one last read through or scan of a document after all changes have been made and to restart that scan from the beginning if you end up making more changes.)

Okay. A few final points. As with bulleted lists you can change the indent and format of your numbered list using the Paragraph dialogue box or the Adjust List Indents option on the dropdown menu.

Also, I mentioned it above, but one thing to be careful of with numbered lists that go into the double-digits or triple-digits is that you can end up with a situation where the text is lined up for values of 1 through 9 but then not aligned once you reach a value of 10 or more.

This can happen, for example, when you use a space instead of a tab to follow the number, but I want to say that I've also seen it happen with tabs if the tabs were set in such a way that it changed which tab stop was used for 1 through 9 versus 10.

Also, it won't be an issue most times, but if you hold your mouse over the numbered list options that Word gives you by default some are right-aligned and some are left-aligned. As you move into larger and large values for your numbered list this may impact the appearance of your list.

To fix this, you'll need to create a New Number Format where you can customize the alignment. That option is at the bottom of the dropdown menu under Define New Number Format. (See screenshot on next page.)

Click on that and it will bring up the Define New Number Format dialogue box where you can choose the number style, number format (whether to use a period or paren or something else even), and the number alignment.

So, for example, the default for 1,2,3 is left-aligned. But you could use this option to make it right-aligned or centered. Here are what those three options look like for numbered values of 9 and 10:

9.   Level 1 Left-Aligned
10. Level 2 Left-Aligned

9.   Level 1 Centered
10.   Level 2 Centered

9.   Level 1 Right-Aligned
10.   Level 2 Right-Aligned

The only change I made here is in the alignment of the numbers. You can see in the first example that the 9 lines up with the 1 in 10. In the second sample it lines up with the center of the 10. And in the third example it lines up with the 0 in the 10. Personally I prefer the right-aligned version. But the default is left-aligned, so the only way to get this is to create your own number format using Define New Number Format.

One nice thing in Word is that once you've used a number format in a document that format is available for you to select again in the Document Number Formats section in the Numbering dropdown menu of the Home tab or the mini formatting menu.

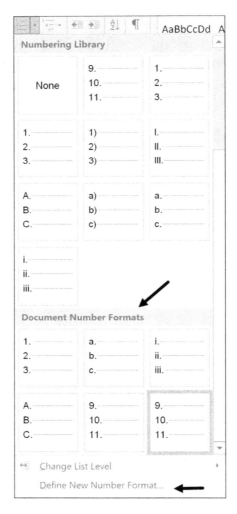

Although one weird thing about that section is that it will show formats you've used at one point but are no longer using. For example, in this screenshot I only have numbered lists in my document right now but it's showing lists with a, b, c, and A, B, C, and I, II, III even though they're not currently in use anywhere in the document.

(One of the reasons I'm careful with playing around with lists in a working document.)

In the case above where I had three different number formats for the 1, 2, 3 numbering you can't tell which is which just from looking. You have to hold your mouse over each one to figure out which one has each alignment.

You could also click on a line that already has that format and see which one of the formats in the dropdown is then surrounded by a dark gray border.

Or you could just use the Format Painter to copy the number formatting over, which is probably what I would actually do instead.

Other Tips & Tricks

Alright. We've talked about how to enter text into Word and how to format that text once you've entered it and how to format your paragraphs. But there are a few more basics we need to cover that don't really have anything to do with entering or formatting your text, although they may lead to changes in your text.

Let's start with Find and Replace.

Find and Replace

Find

If you ever want to find a particular word or phrase in a Word document and you don't want to scan through the whole document, you'll need to use Find. It's very easy to use on the surface, but can also be incredibly powerful if you get into the specialty search options.

For a basic search in Word you can use Ctrl + F or just go to the Navigation task pane on the left-hand side of the workspace. If the Navigation pane is already open then using Ctrl + F will seem like it did nothing, but what it will actually do is place your cursor in the Search Document box in the Results section of the Navigation pane.

(In older versions of Word using Ctrl + F opened the Find and Replace dialogue box so this one throws me every single time.)

If all you're looking for is a simple word or phrase, type it into the search box. You don't even need to hit enter, all instances of the search term will be listed immediately right below the search box. Like so:

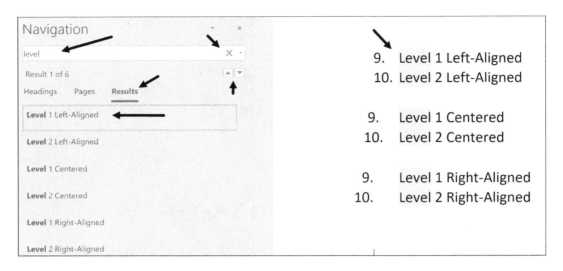

The gray area on the left-hand side is the Navigation pane where I entered "level" as my search term. Immediately below that are the six search results for the document. It bolds the location of the text and provides some of the text around that to make it easy to determine which search result you want.

On the right-hand side is the document itself. Each instance of the search term is highlighted in yellow.

For a larger document where all of the search results are not on the same page, you can simply click on the search result in the list that you want to see and Word will take you to that page. You can also use the up and down arrows just below the far end of the search box (in the same row as the number of search results) to move through your search results one-by-one.

Click on the X at the end of the search box to clear the search result.

Right next to that X is a small dropdown arrow with a list of additional search options. Click on the arrow and one of the first choices is "Advanced Find".

The dropdown is available even if you haven't searched for anything. In that case the X is replaced with a magnifying glass.

Clicking on that Advanced Find option will open the Find and Replace dialogue box which lets you search for far more than just a word or phrase.

I usually get to the same place by using Ctrl + H (which is the control shortcut for replace) and then clicking over to the Find portion of the dialogue box. Either way what you will then see is this:

Type your search phrase into the Find What search bar and then click on Find Next to walk your way through the entire document and look at each instance of your search term.

For a basic search the Navigation pane is the far better choice.

But click on that More button in the bottom left corner of the Find dialogue box and you get this:

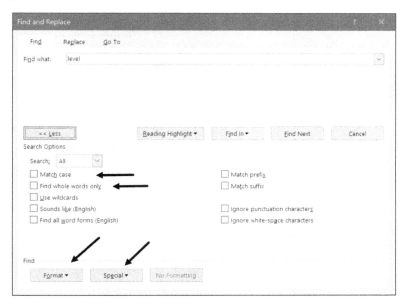

There are a ton of additional search options you can use, but I want to focus on four of them right now.

First, is Match Case. Which is in the Search options section in the middle.

Match Case will look at the search term you enter and only find words with the same capitalization. So if you search for "CAT" and you check this box it will only locate "CAT" for you not "cat" or "Category".

(For my old job something like that would be useful since CAT stood for consolidated audit trail.)

When searching for a proper name or an abbreviation like that, I recommend always checking this box. (This becomes even more important if you're going to use Replace. You wouldn't want to try to replace CAT with some other term and accidentally also replace the cat portion of category with that same term, for example.)

The next option I want to point out is Find Whole Words Only.

Find Whole Words Only will only search for the entire word you enter. So again, with the example of "CAT", if you just searched Word normally it would return any word that has "cat" in it. So "category" and "implication" would be returned along with "CAT" and "cat."

By using Find Whole Words Only the search results would be limited to "CAT" and "cat". You can also combine these two and then your only result would be the one for CAT.

So those are great. And I've saved myself a lot of time over the years by using them.

But a few that I only started using in recent years may be even more powerful than that when they're needed.

At the bottom of the dialogue box are Format and Special dropdown options. Here's what the Format one gives you for choices if you click on it:

A little hard to see maybe, but the options are Font, Paragraph, Tabs, Language, Frame, Style, and Highlight.

Using these options you can search your document for pretty much any format, paragraph style, text style, or highlight that you want. Here's what comes up when you choose Font for example:

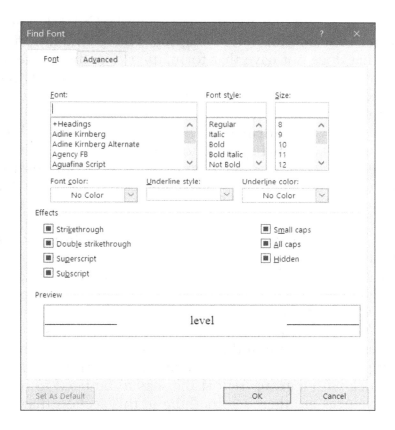

Look at all those options.

Now, that may not sound exciting to you, but let me give you a weird example of where I've needed to use this:

For large-print books they don't use italics, they use bolded text instead. I recently published a seven-hundred-page book in large print. Manually going through that book to find each instance of italics would've been a nightmare. But I was able to easily use find (and replace) to change all of my italics over to bolded text in the space of a minute.

Another time I've needed this is when I've been working on a report and someone decided that all uses of a specific term needed to be in italics or not in italics.Using Format I could search for instances of the term that were not formatted properly. Far easier than looking at every single use of the term one-by-one.

If you know your control shortcuts, you can skip the dropdown and use them directly in the search box.

Just click into the search box and use, for example, Ctrl + I. The first time the search will change to search for that formatting. The second time it will change to search for text that does not have that formatting. The third time it will go back to a neutral search. Which state you're in will show directly below the search box.

To find all text in a document with a specific format, like italics, just leave the search box blank. Don't enter any text. But do use the Ctrl + I or whatever shortcut it is to specify that format. When you click on search Word will show you all of the the text with that specific format.

Also, be careful when using the formatting search options that you don't forget to change your search back to neutral because next time you search you may end up missing a search result. It doesn't happen often, but it has happened to me in the past at least in older versions of Word.

The final one I wanted to point out is right next to the Format option and that is the Special option.

The Special search dropdown allows you to search for specific formatting marks in your document such as paragraph marks, em dashes, en dashes, etc.

This can be a lifesaver if someone gives you a document where they used Enter multiple times instead of using a page break or used tabs to indent paragraphs instead of formatting the paragraph properly.

Maybe most people won't run into needing these options, but if you've ever been the one stuck with a group report that has to be fixed to make everything work properly chances are there's something in this section that will make your life easier.

Replace

Okay. So that's Find which is helpful, but where the real power of Find comes into play is when you pair it with Replace. So not only do you find that italicized text, but you replace it with bolded text at the same time.

Same with fixing two spaces after a period. I was raised to type two spaces after a period but there are members of the younger generation (and even some of my own) who think that using two spaces after a period makes you an archaic fool stuck in the typewriter age. Rather than engage in heated debate about something that really no one should care about, I just used Find and Replace to find all instances of two spaces after a period and replace them with one space.

Easy.

(And I will add that I finally converted from two spaces to one space when I started publishing printed books because when you use justified paragraphs like I am in the print version of this book that extra space after a sentence can created some ugly white space on the page. But honestly, even though I've converted I think it's one of those silly issues people use to distinguish those who are "in the know" from those who are not and I hate that kind of thing with a burning passion. But I digress.)

Back to find and replace. It is fantastic and powerful and will save you so much time. But it's easy to mess up and create horrible and strangely embarrassing errors.

So before you replace every instance of something in your document in one step, make sure that you've thought through what that means.

Let's say I want to replace CAT with SEC CAT. I know I'm not using "cat" in the report I've written, but what about implication, category, catastrophe, etc. If I don't realize that replacing "cat" with "SEC CAT" can affect those words, too, I might be tempted to not constrain my replacements to match the case and to whole words only. In which case I will have SEC CATastrophe in my document somewhere and impliSEC CATion.

Not what you want, so always think it through first.

Okay. So the basics of find and replace:

Use either use Ctrl + H or go to the Editing section of the Home tab and click on Replace to bring up the Find and Replace dialogue box, which will open onto the Replace tab.

The Find What box is the exact same as before and you can click on the More option in the bottom right corner to specify Match Case, Whole Words Only, any formatting, etc. for what you want to find.

There will now be a Replace With box below that where you type what you want to replace that text with. So if CAT needs to become SEC CAT I would type CAT in the Find What box and SEC CAT in the Replace With box. (And be sure to check the whole word and match case boxes as well.)

Another example: If I were replacing two spaces with one I'd type two spaces in the Find What box and one space in the Replace With box.

You then have two choices for how to replace text. You can replace the instances of your search term one one at time by using Find Next and then clicking on Replace once you confirm that you want to use replace. Or you can use Replace All to replace all instances of your search term with your Replace With term at once.

(I recommend double-checking you got it right if you do use Replace All.)

As mentioned above, you can find one type of formatting and replace it with another type of formatting. So I can find italics and replace it with bold, for example. To do this, click into the search and replace boxes and use the relevant control shortcuts for the formatting you want to find and the formatting you want to replace it with.

One other item to note. When Word finds and replaces, it will sometimes do so only from where you are in the document forward. When this happens it tells you how many items it found and replaced and then asks if you want to continue searching from the beginning. To be sure that you've found all instances, say yes.

This means you can also do find and replace on just a highlighted section of text, too, which is sometime very useful. In that instance when it asks if you want it to continue with the rest of the document, say no.

Spelling and Grammar Check

Unless you've done something to your settings or are working in a document that's already hundreds of pages long, you'll notice little red squiggly lines or blue double-underlines appear under some words as you type.

This is Word's real-time spelling and grammar check at work.

To be fair, she wasn't actually trying to pee on her toy, but in Fancyworld there wasn't a good cause and effect connection in place. So it always went: smell something interesting, drop toy to smell it better, step forward to pee on something interesting while forgetting that the toy that was just dropped is right there, too.

I tell ya, that girl keeps me on my toes.

It may be a little hard to see, but in the screenshot above Word flagged Fancyworld and ya as spelling mistakes by placing a squiggly red line under each word and the use of So as a grammar error by placing a double blue line under it.

For spelling errors, right-click and Word will suggest possible spellings at the top of the dropdown menu.

Here, for example, Word suggested using yam, yak, yaw, a, and yet instead of ya. Which actually highlights a key point with using the spelling and grammar check. Word can't always tell what you were trying to do. So in this case "ya" is slang usage for "you" but that never even made the list of suggestions.

The dictionary that Word works from does not contain slang, but when writing fiction, for example, you may find yourself using lots of slang, especially in dialogue. So spellcheck is great and you should use it for every single document you ever give to anyone else, but it has its limits. Do not blindly follow the recommendations.

Not even the grammar recommendations. I have seen the grammar check suggest using its when it's was actually the correct usage. It is not infallible.

But it is helpful.

More so for business or school writing than fiction or casual writing, although you can at least customize your dictionary if you want. In the dropdown shown above you can see that there is an option to Add To Dictionary which if you choose it will add that word to your Word dictionary so that it is never flagged as a misspelling again. (In business settings I will often add my first name to the dictionary because Word flags it every time and wants to change it to something that would not be good in a business setting.)

In general, though, I don't add words to the dictionary. I would rather in each document use the Ignore All choice.

This is mostly because I can't think through every possible usage of a word to make sure there wouldn't be times when it was in fact a misspelling of some other word. For example, what if I had a document that used the word yam in it and I really did misspell it once as ya. I'd miss that if I had added ya to the dictionary.

Bottom line: Don't do something permanent unless you're sure of what you're doing.

A few more things to know about spellcheck:

Sometimes it flags a word as misspelled when it isn't. I've found that I have one or two words in each novel I write that it flags that are genuine words but aren't listed in the default dictionary. I verify the word is spelled and used correctly with a quick internet search before I ignore the error.

Also, if you're not close enough to the right spelling Word can't help you. I used to consistently spell bureaucracy in such a way that it had no idea what word I was trying to write.

For grammar errors, Word will also suggest an immediate fix. I usually leave those until the end when I can run the Spelling and Grammar check on the entire document at once.

And again, sometimes the suggestions it makes aren't the actual problem. For example, above with "so" its suggestion was to keep the so but put a comma after it which to me is simply a different pacing for that sentence that I don't like as much. What it should actually suggest is that I not use so so many times.

(See what I did there? Haha.)

Unless Word has flagged a blatant spelling error I tend not to worry about any of this until I'm done with the entire document and then I run through it all at once. Stopping every single time Word flags a potential issue would bring me out of my writing flow and make me far less efficient. (For those who cannot continue if they know there's an error in what they've already written those lines can be very useful, though.)

Of course, if your document is long enough you will eventually get a message that it had to stop real-time tracking of spelling and grammar errors. I want to say this happens somewhere around one hundred pages.

Okay, then. For those who want to wait until the end and do it all at once, you do not have to scroll through your document and try to find every one of these.

You can use the Spelling & Grammar option which is in the Proofing section of the Review tab on the left-hand side.

Once you click on that option, Word will open a Proofing pane on the right-hand side of your workspace and will show the next grammar or spelling error in the document. (It doesn't automatically start at the top. If you had a selection of text highlighted it will focus on that selected text. If you're clicked somewhere in the document it will work from there forward.)

Here is the result for the grammar error for "so" that we discussed before:

At the top it describes the issue, then it displays a snippet of text around the word or usage that was flagged, and then below that in the Suggestions section shows suggested fixes for the error.

Likewise, here is the Proofing pane for the "ya" spelling error.

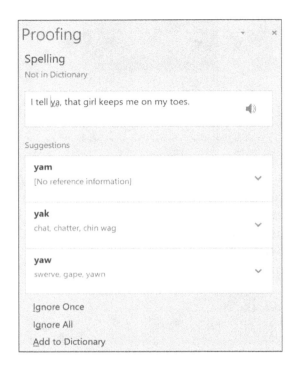

If you agree that there is an error, you can just click on the suggested fix you want and Word will make that edit to your document for you.

If you agree that there's an error but want to fix it some other way, you can click back into your document and make the edit yourself.

If you don't believe there's an error, then at the bottom of the screen you can click on Ignore Once and Word will move on to the next grammar or spelling error.

With spelling errors you can choose to Ignore All and it will not flag that word again in the document but spellcheck sometimes will still flag related uses of a word such as a possessive, singular, plural, or upper or lower case.

For example, it treated all of these as separate words that had to be ignored individually: Winswald Winswalds Winswald's winswald winswald's winswalds.

With grammar errors you can click on Don't Check for This Error. Just be sure that you really want that to happen. Just because it was wrong on this particular instance does not mean it will always be wrong and the listed grammar rules tend to be high-level.

You can see what the grammar error is by looking at the top of the pane. In the case above it says, "After an introductory word or phrase, a comma is best." Before choosing to skip that rule I'd have to believe that there are never any introductory phrases I use where a comma is warranted but I failed to include one. I'm not comfortable deciding that so I'd let it stand.

The final option for spelling in the Proofing page is to add the word to the dictionary, which we already discussed.

The final option for grammar is to see the grammar options. When you click on that choice Word will bring up the Grammar Settings dialogue box.

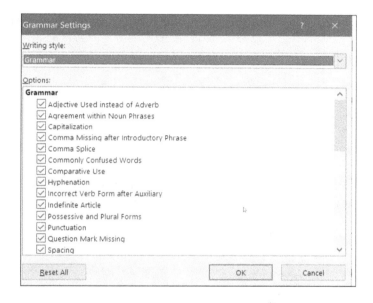

The first screen worth of options are pretty standard and they're all on by default. I don't think any of these give me enough problems that I'd need to turn one off, but you could. The capitalization one can be a little annoying when writing about Excel functions, but otherwise pretty standard stuff.

Where it gets interesting is if you scroll down to the categories for Clarity, Conciseness, Formality, Inclusiveness, Punctuation Conventions, and Vocabulary.

(Now, whether I really want developers who won't use Title Case for their text labels to be telling me about proper word usage is up for debate, but there are some interesting options in those sections.).

For example, in more formal settings, such as academic writing, contractions are frowned upon. The Formality section includes the ability to check your document for those.

So if you are writing an academic paper and want to be sure you didn't accidentally include a contraction, you can have Word check that for you.

There's even a setting for the Oxford comma as well as one for checking for the number of spaces between sentences.

If any of that looks interesting to you, you can go into the Grammar Setup dialogue box and turn those options on by checking the relevant boxes.

Or if one of those rules keeps coming up and you don't want it to, this is the place to fix that.

One final note, once you've run spellcheck on a document and told Word to ignore spelling or grammar errors, it will continue to ignore those errors in that document. To run a clean spelling and grammar check of your document, go to the File tab, click on Options, click on Proofing, and finally click on the gray box labeled Recheck Document.

This will show you a notice that you're about to reset the spelling and grammar check. Click OK and all spelling and grammar errors will be flagged as they were originally.

Synonyms and Thesaurus

In the screenshot above where I showed you the Spelling & Grammar option you may have noticed that there was a Thesaurus option next to it.

A thesaurus, as you may know, is used to identify words with a similar or identical meaning, otherwise known as synonyms.

If I've used "happy" ten times and want to come up with a different word for it, I can use the thesaurus option in Word to find one.

The simplest way to do this is to right-click on the word and go to the synonyms choice in the dropdown menu and then look at the available options listed there:

If you like one of the choices simply click on it and your existing text will be replaced with the chosen word.

You can also select your word and then use the Thesaurus option from the Proofing section of the Review tab to open a Thesaurus task pane on the right-hand side of the workspace.

As you can see, at least in this instance, there are more choices provided in the Thesaurus task pane than there were in the synonyms dropdown menu.

The Thesaurus appears to work differently, however. If you click on one of the words listed it does not replace the word in your document but instead will provide synonyms for that word instead.

To insert the word into your document as a replacement you need to hold your mouse over the word so that it's highlighted, go to the end of the line where that word is, click on the dropdown arrow, and choose insert.

If you had a word or words highlighted in your document it or they will be replaced. If not, the new word will be inserted into the document where your cursor was.

Let me just step back for a moment and give a general caution about using a thesaurus. It's fantastic when what you're doing is triggering your memory of other similar words and you can go down the list and think about each one like a puzzle piece that you're trying to fit into place with what you're writing.

But it is a very bad idea to use a thesaurus to find words you don't already know.

For example, here with happy. One of the options is blissful. Another is exultant. But both of those convey a level of emotion that is not, in my mind, equivalent to being happy. And pleasant, which is another suggested word goes in the wrong direction. Someone is a pleasant person to be around but that is not the same thing as their being a happy person. One is what I feel around that person, another is what they feel.

(If that makes sense. I don't write dictionaries, so forgive me if my example there was bad.) The point is, you have to still know the words you choose when using a thesaurus or it's just not going to sound right.

But if you do need to use it, that's how.

Word Count

The other item in the Proofing section of the Review tab that I want to mention is Word Count. When I was in school we always had to hit a page limit, but for short stories and novels and online forms everyone wants to know the word count.

There are two main places you can find this. The first is actually just in the bottom left-hand corner of the Word screen. You can see there what page you're on and your total page count and then right next to that is the total word count for the document. If you highlight a selection of text the word count will change to show X of Y words so that you can see the number of words in your selection (X) as well as the total number of words in the document (Y).

You can also click on the Word Count option in the Proofing section of the Review tab. This will immediately bring up the Word Count dialogue box:

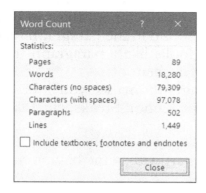

As you can see, it gives a little more information than just word count (which is the second line of information). You also have the number of pages, the number of characters with and without spaces, the number of paragraphs, and the number of lines.

I use the characters option sometimes when I complete online forms that have a character limit but don't tell me how many characters I've used. I type my entry up in Word, check the character count, and then copy it over to the website.

Read Aloud

Just to the right of those three options in the Speech section of the Review tab is the Read Aloud option.

With this option, you can highlight a selection of text in your document, click on Read Aloud, and a computerized voice will read the text to you.

I find this a nice way to review the final draft of my fiction, although it sometimes has very interesting ideas of how to pronounce certain words. For example, grimaced.

Overall, though, it's a good trick to catch those last few straggling errors that the eye tends to skip right over.

(Although not all of them. You never catch them all. I used to write business reports that were reviewed by six people, three of whom were detailed-oriented lawyers who'd gone to schools like Yale and Harvard ,and it never failed that we'd give the client the report and then I'd see a typo that we'd all missed. On page one.)

Show/Hide Paragraph Marks

By default I do not show paragraph and other marks in my document, but when I'm trouble-shooting issues in a document this can be invaluable. The option to show or hide these marks is found in the Paragraph section of the Home tab and is in the top left corner. It looks like a paragraph mark. Click on it to turn on marks, click on it again to turn them off.

Once you turn on paragraph marks you'll be able to see indents, tabs, paragraph breaks, line breaks, section breaks, etc. Like in this example here:

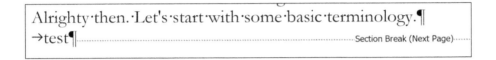

If you look closely you should see a small dot between every single word. That indicates a space. Two dots in a row would indicate two spaces. At the end of every line that uses an Enter there is a paragraph mark. This example has two of those, one after "terminology." in the first line and one after "test" in the second line.

I've also included a tab which is indicated by the arrow on the second line before "test".

And there's a Section Break that will start the next line of text on the next page which is marked with a dashed line and text describing the type of break.

Showing paragraph marks is useful for finding those little annoyances like tabs or extra enters or a page or section break somewhere it wasn't supposed to be. You can often guess that they're there, but this is the only surefire way to know exactly what you're dealing with.

* * *

Alright, next we're going to cover some of the customized settings available under the Options section of the File tab.

File Options Customized Settings

Click on the File tab and then choose Options from the left-hand side and this will bring up the Word Options dialogue box which has a number of categories for options you can customize.

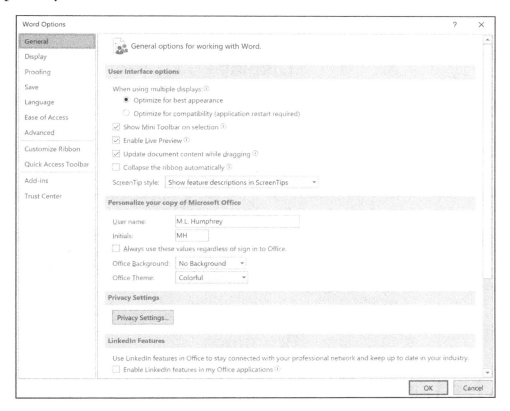

I'm not going to cover everything you can do here because there are easily over a hundred different settings, but I will point out some of the ones I've needed to use in the past.

General

The main change I've needed to make here is in the Personalize Your Copy of Microsoft Office section. As you can see in the screenshot above it defaults to showing my initials as MH, but I've in the past been on work teams where someone else had those same initials and that can be problematic for track changes. So this is where to adjust that to MLH for me, for example.

It also shows the ability to change the user name, but I want to say that I had to go into BIOS or somewhere to actually change my name to my initials for Office. So you can try it here, but it may not work or it may not hold for anything other than track changes. Be sure to check the box that says to always use those values regardless of sign in to Office, but then be careful if you have multiple users on the same computer.

(Basically, if this matters for you, double-check that it's working properly before you send the document off or take screenshots.)

Display

It looks like it's the default in Word 2019, but I always make sure that it says show white space between pages in print layout view. Without this box checked, you can't visually see page breaks in your document, one page of text rolls right into the next with just a thin gray line to indicate a page break.

That's especially annoying if you're working with a document that has very short sections that are supposed to fall on their own page because you can end up with three or four of them displayed on a single page.

I never customize the section that asks to show formatting marks on the screen because I only turn that on when I need that as discussed above, otherwise I want them hidden. But if find that you have marks showing in a document that won't turn off, check here to see if someone changed the settings so that some marks would be permanently visible.

Proofing

The Proofing section allows you to control when Word applies its AutoCorrect options and which ones it applies.

This one I always make changes to. (I haven't yet on this version of Word because I wanted to write this book first and it's driving me crazy to deal with the defaults.)

AutoCorrect Options

Most of the changes I make in this section are under the AutoCorrect Options. I click on that button and it brings up the AutoCorrect dialogue box which has five available tabs. I use the AutoCorrect, AutoFormat as You Type, and AutoFormat tabs to make adjustments.

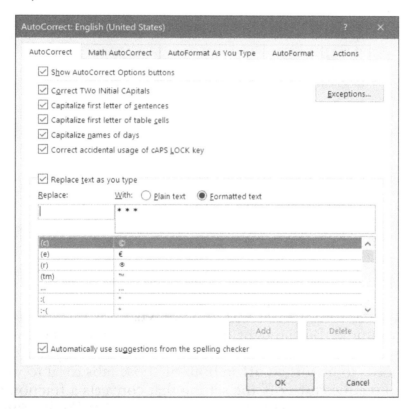

For example, at my old job on the AutoCorrect tab I would always delete that first option to change (c) into the copyright sign because my job involved a lot of rule citations, where you write things like Rule 3070(c) which made it really annoying each time Word automatically changed that over to a copyright sign.

Your other option is to use Ctrl + Z when Word makes a correction you don't want. (My problem is that I'm usually about three words past the change before

I realize what's happened. At that point it becomes more of a hassle than it's worth.)

The AutoFormat As You Type and AutoFormat tabs include the setting for smart quotes versus straight quotes, which is another one I often change.

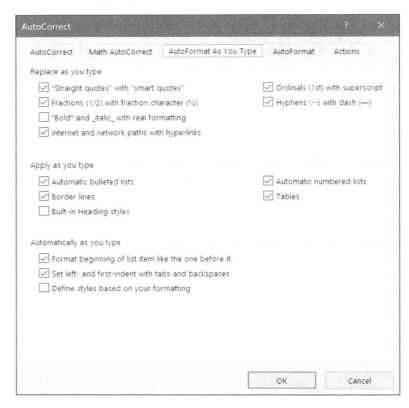

Smart quotes curve towards the text and are what you're supposed to use for dialogue, for example. But straight quotes are what you need to use in Excel formulas. So when I'm writing my Excel books I usually turn this one off.

It actually needs to be turned off in both of those tabs for it to work properly.

I will also sometimes turn off the setting that converts a fraction and the one that automatically creates hyperlinks, depending on what I'm working on.

Now, don't get me wrong. A lot of the autocorrect options are very handy—I often type too fast and mistype "the" as "teh" and Word always catches that for me—but do keep an eye out for "errors" you don't want fixed as you type like turning a single i into a capital I.

The AutoCorrect dialogue box is also where you can see that Word will automatically convert two dashes in a row into an em-dash.

(But only after you type a word, two dashes, another word, and a space.)

This is also where you can see that three periods in a row will turn into an ellipsis which treats them as one single character and keeps them together.

If you like to learn shortcuts or ways to make life easier that it's probably worth looking through these tabs to know what Word will do on your behalf so you can leverage it.

But if you're more like me then you'll probably wait to look at this section until you get annoyed with something that keeps happening that you want to turn off.

Check Spelling As You Type

In the third section of the Proofing screen you can uncheck the box that says to check spelling as you type so that you no longer have to see those red squiggly lines under words.

Mark Grammar Errors As You Type

Same for grammar errors. You can uncheck the box for that option to turn that off so that you aren't seeing the blue double underline in your document as you type.

This is also the section for turning off the grammar check altogether. Uncheck Check Grammar With Spelling and Word will no longer check for grammar when you select the Spelling and Grammar option on the Review tab.

Reset Spelling and Grammar Check

As mentioned previously, you can click on Recheck Document to reset the spelling and grammar check for the document. If you checked the document previously and told it to ignore errors but want to see those errors now, this is the way to do that.

Save

Prior to Word 2019 I would have recommended saving documents as a .doc instead of the default format which is .docx to ensure backward compatibility. Versions of Word from 2007 onward use .docx as their default but it's a format that users of Word versions prior to that can't open.

We're probably now in the safe range where most users have upgraded to new enough versions of Word that this isn't a concern. But if it ever is and you don't want to have to think about it you can change the default file format that Word uses to save your documents here.

This is also where you can specify how often Word saves an AutoRecovery version of your file. The default is set to 10 minutes. If you're ever working in Word and it crashes on you, then when you reopen that file in Word it will offer to let you open the recovery version instead which by default was saved at some point in the last ten minutes.

Word does not crash on me often, but when it does this has been a lifesaver for me. (More often it's that my entire computer crashed on me, not just Word.)

Normally the AutoRecovery process is so seamless you won't even notice it's happening, but I do have a set of formatted templates I work with that for some reason take long enough to save that they will freeze my computer for a minute or so as they save. Having that happen every ten minutes can be annoying, to say the least, so when working with them I will sometimes adjust this setting.

This section also lets you choose your default location for saving files, so if you always want to save to an X drive or something, this is where to change that setting.

Advanced

There are many options in this section. I can see a few that might be useful to change, like unchecking the allow text to be dragged and dropped option since I don't do that intentionally but have had it happen a few times unintentionally.

This is also the section where if you're going to work with documents that need high resolution images for print you'll want to change the default. Otherwise all of your images, no matter what their quality is when you bring them into Word will be 220 dpi which is generally considered too low for printing standards.

Customize Ribbon

The Customize Ribbon option lets you choose which tasks are available at the top of the screen in your Word workspace. So, for example, the options under the Home tab.

I would advise against this unless you work for yourself and have no expectation that you will ever use anyone else's computer or any public computer. Because what makes things faster for you in your version will significantly slow you down on anyone else's computer.

Also, you'll have to do this again with any new version of Word you buy which means another significant slowdown every couple of years as you upgrade to a new software version.

Not to mention, if you get stuck no one else will have the display you do so you'll be on your own trying to figure out where something is.

Quick Access Toolbar

Customizing the Quick Access Toolbar, on the other hand, makes a lot of sense if there are just one or two tasks that you use often that are located in a tab other than the one you usually need.

For me, for example, I usually put Breaks and Format Painter here so that I can access those from wherever I am.

File Info

We just discussed the File Options choices, but there's another section of the File tab that I want to explore and that's the Info section.

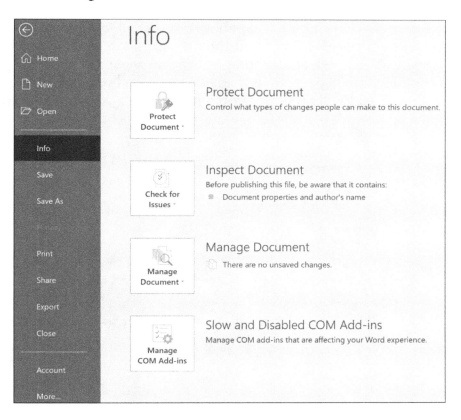

You reach it by clicking on the File tab and then the Info option on the left-hand side of the screen.

One of the things you can do here is strip the document of any personal information. So the author name, any track changes, any comments, etc. There are definitely times this is called for and you should always check a document for track changes before you hand it off to a client or professor or some other person who wasn't meant to see your comments and changes.

(I've been on the receiving end a few times of documents where that didn't happen and let's just say that you don't want to give you regulator the track changes version of your response to their inquiry...)

Which means it's a useful and necessary thing to be able to do. BUT. I hesitate to tell you about it because when used at the wrong time it can be a disaster. I have had people strip out the author information on a working document and then every single person's comments were listed as "Author" even if those comments were added after that point in time. So be careful with this, please.

Okay. The way you review a document for information you might want to remove is by clicking on the Check for Issues box next to where it says Inspect Document. From that dropdown then choose Inspect Document.

(You can see that this also gives you the option to Check Compatibility with older versions of Word, too, should that ever be an issue.)

When you choose to inspect the document Word will prompt you to save it if you haven't already and will then give you a list of categories it can scan for:

I usually scan for everything. When the scan is done it will display another dialogue box with any issues it found and let you choose which issues to fix:

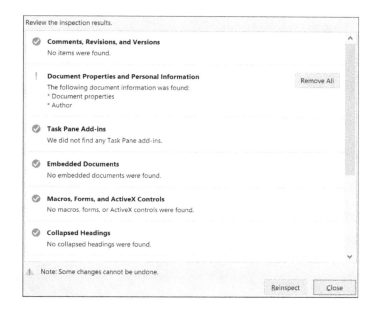

BE VERY CAREFUL at this point that you don't remove something you will need and can't get back. (Like author information in a working document.)

What I recommend is that you save a copy of the file before you inspect it and then save the inspected and stripped down version as a new file. That way if you did delete something you shouldn't, you can go back and fix it.

That's basically all I use this section for, but as I mentioned above you can check for compatibility with older versions of Word.

You can also protect the document so that people can't edit it and password protect the document so that no one can open unless they have the password. (Just be sure you remember your password or you won't be able to open the file either.)

Okay. Now we're up to printing a document. But before we can print we need to know how to format the page so that it has page numbers and headers and footers. So let's cover that next.

Page Formatting

If you're going to print a document that is more than one page long, chances are you'll want to add page numbering to the document as well as maybe a header or footer that includes the document title or your name or both. Let's talk about how to do that.

Page Numbering

First, do not ever manually number your pages. Word will do this for you. By letting Word do this, you ensure that the page numbering will still work even when you make edits to the document.

Nothing worse than putting a 1 at the bottom of what you think is page one and then deciding to add a title to the document and suddenly there's a random 1 in the middle of the second page.

So don't do that. Please.

(Says the person who has occasionally been stuck fixing a document where someone did in fact do this. That and the person who manually formatted the text to *look* like track changes...Took me ages to realize what that person had done. And even longer to fix it. But you're reading this book so you won't do that kind of thing, right? Right.)

To add page numbers to your document, go to the Header & Footer section of the Insert tab which is towards the right-hand side, and click on the arrow next to Page Number.

This will bring up a dropdown menu that lets you choose where on the page you want your page numbers to display. If you hold your mouse over those options, you can then choose how you want those page numbers to look.

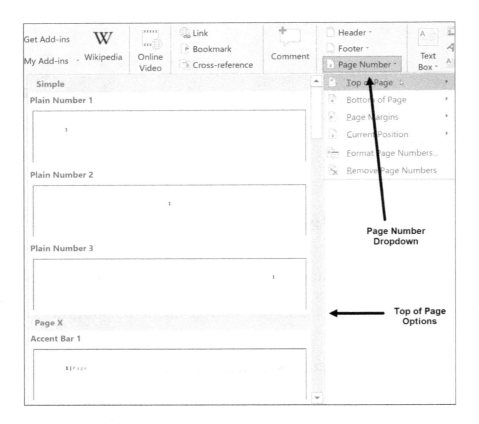

Above I've held my mouse over Top of Page and you can see the first four options I have to choose from, left, middle, right, and a left-hand accented option. If I scroll down in that list there are actually twenty-five total options to choose from some of which are quite distinctive.

Click on the choice you want and Word will insert it into the header (for top of page) or footer (for bottom of page). If you choose the page margins options, that is inserted into a standalone text box on the side of the page.

Current Position will insert the page number where your cursor currently is, so I'd only use that one if you already have a header or footer in your document (or a text box you want to use) and you're clicked into that space.

The Format Page Number option in that dropdown can be used to change the numbering format (to small case Roman numerals for example), the starting page number, or to specify that the numbering should or should not continue from a prior section. (This becomes much more relevant when you have sections in your document that require separate numbering. I cover how to create sections in *Word 2019 Intermediate*.)

For a basic simple page number using the dropdown menu and choosing one of the defaults should really be all you have to do.

Headers and Footers

Inserting a page number is basically a specialized version of inserting a header or footer. When you insert the page number at the top of the page or the bottom of the page Word creates a space that is separate from your main text and puts the page number there. But you can also put other text into the header or footer like your name or the title of the document.

Doing so will repeat that text at the top or bottom of the page for the entire document. (Or section if you're using sections. Also, you can set it up so that alternating pages have different text in them like a book does. But for basic headers and footers it repeats throughout the document.)

A header goes at the top of your page.

A footer goes at the bottom of your page.

To add one, go to the Header & Footer section of the Insert tab and click on the arrow below the one you need (header or footer), and then choose the option that works best for you, just like you did with page numbering.

Just like with page numbering you will have various pre-formatted options to choose from like these three for the footer:

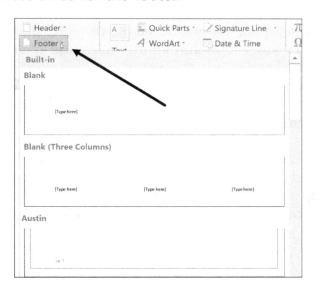

You're not stuck with the format you choose. For example, with short story submissions, they usually want the header to be in the top right corner. If you choose the Blank header option, that creates a header that's in the top left corner. But you can simply go to the Home tab and choose to right-align the text in your header and that will put it in the right corner instead.

After you choose your header or footer option, Word creates a header or footer and inserts [Type here] into the designated spots where you're supposed to put text.

To edit that text, just start typing because it will already be highlighted in gray. If it isn't highlighted in gray, select the text and then start typing.

Text in your header or footer works just like text in your document. You can use the same options from the Home tab to change your font, font size, color, etc.

As mentioned above, headers and footers are in a separate area from the main text of your document. If you're in a header or footer and want to go back to the main document, you can (1) double-click back onto the main body of your document, (2) click on Close Header and Footer in the menu bar which should be showing in the Design tab under Header & Footer Tools, or (3) hit the Esc key on your keyboard.

If you're in your main document and want to edit your header or footer, you can (1) double-click on the text in the header or footer, or (2) right-click on the header or footer and choose "Edit Header" or "Edit Footer" from the dropdown.

Margins

Margins are the white space along the edges of your document. The default margins in Word 2019 are one-inch margins all around which is pretty standard so you probably won't have to edit this often.

But if you need to edit your margins, you can go to the Layout tab and under the Page Setup section click on the dropdown under Margins. This will give you the choice of Normal, Narrow, Moderate, Wide, Mirrored, Office 2003 Default, and Custom Margins.

Mirrored margins are for printed texts where the inside margins are the same for facing pages and the outside margins are the same for facing pages. (As opposed to thinking about the left-hand margin and the right-hand margin which is what you think about with a report or other printed document that is seen one single page at a time.)

Each option, except Custom Margins, shows what the margins are for that option.

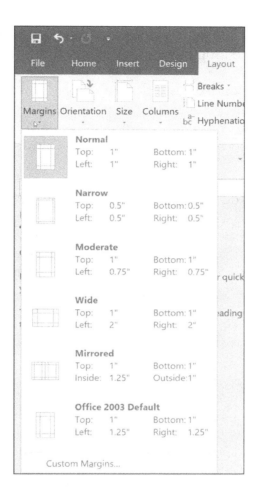

Clicking on Custom Margins, will open the Page Setup dialogue box directly onto the Margins tab. You can also open the Page Setup dialogue box to the Margins tab by clicking on the expansion arrow for the Page Setup section.

This lets you specify a custom value for each margin as well as for the document gutter. (Which matters if you're printing book-style.) In the Pages section dropdown you can also specify that the margins should be mirrored.

Page Orientation

A standard document has a page orientation of portrait. That's where the long edge of the document is along the sides and the short edge is across the bottom and top. This is how most books, business reports, and school papers are formatted, and it's the default in Word.

But sometimes you'll create a document where you need to turn the text ninety degrees so that the long edge is at the top and bottom and the short edge is on the sides.

A lot of tables in appendixes are done this way. Also presentation slides are often this way. That's called landscape orientation.

(Think paintings here. A drawing of a person—a portrait—is generally taller than it is wide. A drawing of a mountain range—a landscape—is generally wider than it is tall.)

To change the orientation of your document, go to the Page Setup section of the Layout tab, click on the arrow under Orientation, and choose the orientation you want.

If you use section breaks--which are covered in *Word 2019 Intermediate*—you can set the page orientation on a section-by-section basis. But if you're not using sections, changing the orientation on any page will change the orientation of the entire document so be careful with this one.

You can also change the orientation in the Page Setup dialogue box which can be opened via the expansion arrow for the Page Setup section. The orientation option is on the Margins tab directly below the Margins settings.

Printing

Printing in Word, at its most basic, is incredibly easy. You can simply type Ctrl + P or go to File and choose Print from the list of options on the left-hand side. Both options will bring you to the Print screen.

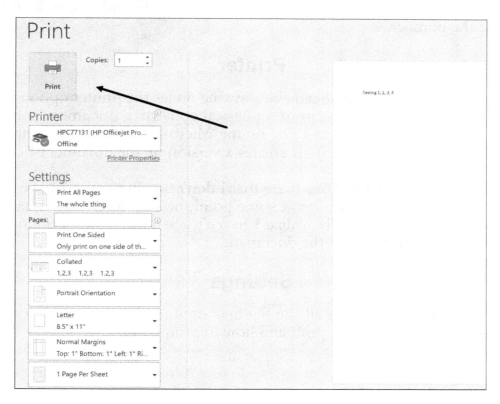

If all you want is to print the document with no adjustments, click on the printer image (see screenshot above) that's directly below where it says Print.

A lot of times this should be fine. It's not like Excel where you really need to check what it's going to look like because in Word as you were working you could see what it was going to look like.

But just in case, on the right-hand side Word will show you a preview of what the document will look like when it prints. For documents that are longer than a page, you can use the arrows at the bottom to navigate through the document preview.

There are a number of adjustments you can make before you print that will impact what prints and how.

Let's walk through those now from top to bottom.

Copies

Right next to the Print icon you can specify the number of copies you want to print. The default is one copy. To increase that amount, either click into the box and type a new number or use the arrows on the right-hand side to increase or decrease the number.

Printer

Your default printer should already be showing under the printer option.

Sometimes I don't want to print a physical copy of a document and so I'll choose the Microsoft Print to PDF or the Microsoft XPS Document Writer option instead of my printer. This creates a version of the document I can save to my computer.

There are a few other options there that I don't use, but you may, like fax.

If you do change your printer at some point, be sure to change it back next time you go to print. I usually realize I haven't when instead of printing Word asks me where I want to save the document.

Settings

Below the printer choice are all the Settings options that let you choose what portions of the document to print and how to print them.

Print All Pages Or Other Page Selections

The first choice you have is what portion of the document to print. The default is Print All Pages which will print the entire document.

If you click on that dropdown, however, there are a number of other choices. Print Selection will print any text that you have selected in the document.

Print Current Page will print the page you were clicked onto when you chose to print. You can verify that it's the right page in the print preview to the right.

Custom Print uses the pages box directly below the dropdown. You can type in the specific pages you want there. For page ranges, use a dash. For a list of individual pages, use commas.

So if you want to print pages 3, 5, and 7 you would enter "3,5,7" in the Pages box. If you wanted to print pages 3 through 7, you would enter "3-7" in the box.

If you go directly to the pages box and start typing in a page range it will automatically change the dropdown to "Custom Print."

You can also print in Word 2019 the Document Info, List of Markup which is your tracked changes, a list of the styles being used in the document, a list of items in your autotext gallery, and a list of any custom shortcut keys you have.

You can also choose to print only odd pages or only even pages.

And there's a choice to print the document with markup.

Print One-Sided or Two-Sided

The default is for Word to print on one side of the page, but you can change it to print two-sided documents.

To do so, click on the arrow next to the default choice of one-sided. You'll now see a dropdown with four options, one-sided, both sides with the long edge, both sides with the short edge, and manually print on both sides.

Choose the manual option if you have a printer that isn't set up to print two-sided documents automatically.

Choose to flip pages on the long edge for documents with a portrait orientation. Choose to flip pages on the short edge for documents with a landscape orientation.

Collation

This is only relevant if you're printing more than one copy of a document that's more than one page long.

The default when printing multiple copies of a document is to print one entire copy of the document and then print the next copy of the document. (That's the *collated* option that shows 1,2,3 1,23 1,2,3.)

The other option you can choose is to print all of your page ones and then all of your page twos and then all of your page threes. (That's the *uncollated* option that shows 1,1,1 2,2,2, 3,3,3)

The uncollated option is useful for situations where you might be giving out handouts one page at a time, but generally you'll want to stick with collated copies.

Orientation

We talked about this one before, but if you want the text on your page to go across the long edge instead of across the short edge, this is another place where you can make that choice.

The default is Portrait Orientation, but if you click on the arrow, you can instead choose Landscape Orientation.

Paper Size

The default in Word (at least in the U.S. version) is to print on 8.5"x11" paper. If you want to print your document on a different size of paper (say A4 or legal), then this is where you'd change that setting.

There are an insane number of choices both on the dropdown menu and if you click on More Paper Sizes, but for most documents you'll probably be using the default.

Make sure you have whatever paper you end up choosing if you're printing to an actual printer.

Margins

We already talked about how to change the margins on your document, but this is also another place where you can do that. You have the same pre-formatted margin choices here as in the Layout tab as well as the custom option.

Pages To Print Per Sheet

If you want to save paper because perhaps you're reviewing a document and it's not the final version, you can print more than one page of your document onto a single sheet.

The default is to print one page on one sheet, but if you click on the dropdown menu you can choose to print 2, 4, 6, 8, or 16 pages per sheet.

You can also choose to scale your text to a chosen paper size.

Be careful with this setting because Word will let you make a choice that results in an illegible document. Four pages on one page is still legible, but I suspect that sixteen pages on one page would be a challenge for most people to read. (But it may be useful if you're ever in a situation where your teacher said you could bring one page of notes and you're trying to cram an entire semester's worth of knowledge on that one page...)

Page Setup

As a beginner, I'd ignore the Page Setup link at the bottom of the page. Most of what it covers we've already addressed above. It's just the older way of specifying your print settings.

Conclusion

Alright. There you have it. Enough knowledge about Word to let you do most of what you need to do on a daily basis.

If you want to learn more, in *Word 2019 Intermediate* I dive into how to create complex numbered lists, insert tables, use section breaks, insert a table of contents, use styles, add watermarks and hyperlinks, deal with track changes, and more. Things that you may need to do at some point, but aren't essential to get started with Word.

You don't have to continue with that book, though. Word also has excellent help available.

The first option is to hold your mouse over any of the options in the menu at the top, like here for Format Painter. This will give you a basic description of what the option does as well as list any control shortcut that exists for it.

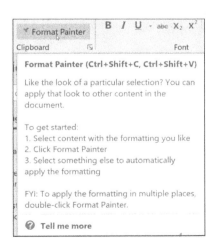

Many of the options will include Tell Me More at the bottom. You can click on that and it will open the Help task pane to a help pane specific to that topic.

You can also click on Help under the Help tab. This will open the Help task pane as well but to a generic starter screen where you can then browse the subject categories or search for what you're trying to do.

The Help tab also has a Show Training option which brings up a list of topics where you can then watch videos on each of the listed topics which can be helpful in learning something new.

If none of that works I will often do an internet search for what I'm looking for using "microsoft word" as part of my search string. So I might search for "how to add a hyperlink microsoft word." I then choose the support.microsoft. com option.

That's an excellent resource for how things work, but sometimes I need "is this possible" help, in which case I'll look to user forums to see if anyone else has asked my question before. (I find I need this less with Word than with Excel, though.)

You can also email me at mlhumphreywriter@gmail.com. I'm happy to point you in the right direction or figure out the answer myself and share it if I don't already know it. Sometimes it's just a matter of knowing the right buzz words to use to ask the question.

Okay. So that's it. Good luck with it! Don't let it scare you. If you're nervous then save drafts of what you're working on so you can go back to a prior version that was working for you. But generally just take it slow and easy and you should be fine. Especially if you stick to the basics we covered here.

Control Shortcuts

The following is a list of useful control shortcuts in Word. For each one, hold down the Ctrl key and use the listed letter to perform the command.

Command	Ctrl +
Bold	B
Center	E
Copy	C
Cut	X
Find	F
Italicize	I
New	N
Paste	V
Print	P
Redo	Y
Replace	H
Save	S
Select All	A
Underline	U
Undo	Z

INDEX

A

Arrow 8

AutoCorrect Options 74–76

AutoFormat 76–77

AutoRecovery Settings 78

B

Bold Text 29–31

Bulleted Lists 43–46

C

Click 4

Clipboard 19

Close a File 16

Control Shortcuts 9–10, 99

Copy 19–20

Copy Formatting 32

Cursor 8

Customize Ribbon 78

Customized Settings 73

Cut 19–20

D

Delete a File 15

Delete Text 18

Dialogue Box 6

DOC File Type 14

DOCX File Type 14, 77

Dropdown Menu 5

E

Expansion Arrow 6

F

File Info 81–83

File Options 73

Find 55–56, 58–60

Fonts 23

Choice 23–24

Color 27–28

Selecting 24–26

Size 26–27

Footers 87–88

Format Painter 32–33, 39

G

Grammar Check 62–68

H

Headers 87–88

Help 97–98

Highlight 4

Highlight, Add to Text 28–29

I

Images, High Resolution Settings 78

Italicize Text 30–31

L

Left-Click 4

M

Margins 88–89, 94

N

New File 11–12

Numbered Lists 47–53

O

Open a File 12

Orientation, Page 89–90

P

Page Formatting 85

Page Numbers 85–86

Paragraph Marks 72

Paragraphs 35

Alignment 35–37

Indenting 41–43

Line Spacing 37, 38

Spacing Between 39–41

Paste 19–21

Paste Options 21, 22

Printing 91

Collated 93–94

Copies 92

One-Sided versus Two-Sided 93

Orientation 94

Pages Per Sheet 94

Paper Size 94

Print 92

Print Pages Selection 93

Printer Choice 92

Proofing Pane 66

Q

Quick Access Toolbar 9

Quick Access Toolbar, Customize 79

R

Read Aloud 71

Redo 18

Remove Identifying Information 82

Rename a File 15

Replace 60–62

Right-Click 4

S

Save a File 13–15

Save As 14–15

Save Options 77

Scroll Bar 7–8

Search *See Also Find*

Select 4

Spellcheck 62–67

Synonyms 69

T

Tab 3

Task Pane 7

Text Format 28

Thesaurus 69–70

U

Underline Text 30–31

Undo 17

User Name, Change 74

W

White Space Between Pages 74

Word Count 70–71

About the Author

M.L. Humphrey is a former stockbroker with a degree in Economics from Stanford and an MBA from Wharton who has spent close to twenty years as a regulator and consultant in the financial services industry.

You can reach M.L. Humphrey at:

mlhumphreywriter@gmail.com

or at

www.mlhumphrey.com

www.ingramcontent.com/pod-product-compliance
Lightning Source LLC
Chambersburg PA
CBHW060159060326
40690CB00018B/4173